The Confederate Navy
A Study in Organization

Winner in 1969 of the Mrs. Simon Baruch University Award, made by the United Daughters of the Confederacy for the best unpublished book or monograph of high merit in the field of Southern History in or near the period of the Confederacy or bearing upon the causes that led to secession and the War Between the States.

Baruch Awards 1927-1960

1927—Carpenter, J. T., *The South as a Conscious Minority 1789–1861*.

1929—Whitfield, T. M., *Slavery Agitation in Virginia 1829–1832*.

1931—Flanders, Ralph Betts, *Plantation Slavery in Georgia*.

1933—Thompson, Samuel Bernard, *Confederate Purchasing Agents Abroad*.

1935—Wiley, Bell Irvin, *Southern Negroes 1861–1865*.

1937—Hill, Louise Biles, *Joseph E. Brown and the Confederacy*.

1940—Haydon, F. S., *Aeronautics of the Union and Confederate Armies*.

1942—Stormont, John, *The Economic Stake of the North in the Preservation of the Union in 1861*.

1945—Schultz, Harold Sessel, *Nationalism and Sectionalism in South Carolina 1852–1860*.

1948—Tankersley, A. P., *John Brown Gordon: Soldier and Statesman*.

1951—Todd, Richard Cecil, *Confederate Finance*.

1954—Morrow, Ralph E., *Northern Methodism and Reconstruction*.

1954—Cunningham, Horace, *Doctors in Gray*.

1957—Hall, M. H., *The Army of New Mexico: Sibley's Campaign of 1862*.

1960—Robertson, James I. Jr., *Jackson's Stonewall: A History of The Stonewall Brigade*.

The Confederate Navy ∽ A STUDY IN ORGANIZATION

by Tom Henderson Wells

Winner of the Mrs. Simon Baruch
University Award of
The United Daughters of the Confederacy

THE UNIVERSITY OF ALABAMA PRESS
University, Alabama

Contents

Foreword

T H I S study of the Confederate Navy is a study in failure. Unlike the Confederate Army, the Navy had few moments of triumph and ever fewer hopes of final success. From the first, its officers were either pessimistic or silent concerning the possibilities of victory. Stephen R. Mallory, Secretary of the Navy, and Raphael Semmes were among the few who ever intimated that they could do more than postpone defeat. Yet the country was committed to a grimly industrial war in which the sea and rivers must play a very important part. This work is concerned primarily with the navy's organizational structure—its origin, components, and functions. It also deals with persons who held key positions in the organization and the manner in which they discharged the duties for which they were responsible. It treats only incidentally of naval operations. The writer's original intention was to prepare a full history of the Confederate Navy, but as he delved into the subject he found that no one had ever prepared a detailed description of the organization and duties of the navy department and its subordinate agencies. This information had to be laboriously assembled from manuals, registers, reports, correspondence, and other primary sources. Now that it is compiled, it will serve as an essential preliminary to the definitive history still to be written.

Secretary Mallory regarded possible abolitionist raids as the first seaborne threat to the Confederacy. A second problem which he recognized soon after the war started was that the Confederate Navy was unlikely ever to match the United States Navy ship for ship. Mallory therefore decided to build a few powerful, relatively invulnerable vessels. The Confederacy lacked the time, money, and technical ability to construct complicated vessels at home; so with whatever money it could raise, it would have to buy them or have them built abroad.

The advent of the blockade presented him with a third problem, which finally fixed Mallory's naval policy. He wanted heavily armored steam vessels mounting a few very heavy guns. With these ironclads he would sweep aside or sink Union blockaders and bombard Northern coastal cities into submission. At the same time, faster, lightly armed cruisers would open Southern harbors to world trade by drawing off blockading vessels, and would bankrupt Yankee traders and fishermen by destroying their ships.

From the beginning Mallory's policy had little if any chance of success. In the first place, no foreign nation had a seagoing ironclad for sale. An armament race between France and England had begun in 1857 with the construction of the *Gloire* and the *Warrior*. Both nations experienced difficulties in solving the new problems created by their innovations, but by 1861 each had a number of ironclads on the ways and neither felt it could allow the other to gain a superiority. Other European countries lacked technological capabilities and facilities to build ironclads. In any case the Confederacy would have to wait at least a year for such a ship to be built.

In the second place, there was the problem of getting new warships to sea. The British Foreign Enlistment Act forbade the outfitting and sailing of armed expeditions from home waters. Before the development of ironclads there was so little difference between warships and commercial vessels that it was possible to evade these rules, as well as international custom. Mallory was completely in line with dominant Confederate opinion when he relied upon British interest in Southern cotton to provide both diplomatic and financial assistance. And Napoleon III in

France, although he had shown every sign of cooperating with the Confederacy, elected to follow the British example and avoid involvement in the American conflict. Mallory never quite accepted as fact the failure of his European building program, and he kept devising stop-gaps calculated to keep the Confederacy alive until his great scheme could be realized.

Mallory had no policy for the defense of rivers, and he never developed one. In this important area his naval assistants gave him no help; they did not consider that protection of inland waters was within their province. They recognized a responsibility for water-borne harbor defenses, but rivers, shore batteries, and forts (in their view) belonged to the army.

Mallory and many of the naval officers had a curiously persistent idea that one of the most important reasons for having a wartime navy was to provide the basis for a postwar establishment. This illogical notion was most clearly revealed in correspondence about the education of midshipmen, but it also was manifested in opposition to the sale of Confederate ships detained in Europe, and the existence of two overlapping corps of officers.

As the war progressed, the Confederate Navy was forced to react to enemy naval activity, regardless of its own objectives and means. By the end of 1862 the Union Navy had passed the shakedown phase, but the Confederate Navy was forced into ever greater improvisations. The domestic policy thus imposed on the South was to build, operate, and maintain naval forces capable in conjunction with army forces of repelling water-borne attack.

Whatever its merits or faults, this imposed policy formed the background against which Confederate naval organization must be judged.

The Confederate Navy
A Study in Organization

1

The Navy Department

T H E Confederate Constitution provided for the establishment of a navy. The Provisional Congress continued in effect all Federal laws, rules, and regulations that were not inconsistent with the Confederate Constitution, and created executive departments, including the Navy Department. This act provided for a Secretary of the Navy who should, under the direction and control of the president, have charge of the navy.[1] A subsequent act passed 16 March 1861 provided for four offices within the Navy Department: the first was charged with responsibility for matters of ordnance and hydrography; the second was responsible for preparation and issuance of orders and detail and of legal matters; the third had medical responsibilities; the fourth was in charge of acquiring provisions, clothing, and coal. The act also established a Marine Corps within the Navy Department.[2]

The Navy was heir not only to organizational material from the U.S. Navy, but also to its customs and traditions. However, specific division of responsibility at the highest level differed notably from that which had been effective in the United States Navy since 1842. The United States Navy Department included Bureaus of Yards and Docks;

---

1. United States Navy Department, comp., *Official Records of the Union and Confederate Navies in the War of the Rebellion* (Washington, 1894–1922), ser. 2, II, 44. Hereafter cited as *O.R.N.*
2. Confederate States Navy Department, comp., *Register of the Commissioned and Warrant Officers of the Navy of the Confederate States to January 1, 1864* (Richmond, 1864), 61–62. Hereafter cited as *C. S. Navy Register 1864.*

Construction, Equipment, and Repair; Provisions and Clothing; Ordnance and Hydrography; and Medicine and Surgery. An Engineer in Chief, with assistants, was attached to the Bureau of Construction, Equipment, and Repair.[3]

In the United States Navy, the office of the Secretary managed personnel matters and it was necessary for officers, even of junior grades, to apply directly to the secretary for duty. The inclusion in Confederate Navy Department organization of the Office of Orders and Detail was an improvement over that of the United States Navy.

The Confederate Navy Department organization was defective in failing to provide responsibility for shore establishments and for the construction, repair, and maintenance of ships and their engines. An unofficial directory to the executive offices published by C. A. Vanfelson, the Navy Department messenger, indicates that in 1861 matters of construction and repair and of yards and docks were referred to the Office of Ordnance and Hydrography and that matters concerning equipment of vessels went to the Office of Orders and Detail.[4] A limited reorganization in the summer of 1863 included the needed establishment of the Chief Constructor and the Engineer in Chief as immediate subordinates of the Secretary of the Navy. All other equipment of vessels except ordnance was officially assigned to the Office of Orders and Detail, as was the duty of maintaining supplies of coal.[5]

Although Confederate law established a separate office to handle naval personnel matters, change of duty orders were issued in the name of the Secretary. The Secretary was responsible for orders of an operational nature. The Secretary, as head of an executive department, was authorized to address congress or to attend its sessions. He was responsible for presenting congress with itemized requests for

---

3. United States Navy Department, comp., *Register of the Commissioned and Warrant Officers of the Navy of the United States including Officers of the Marine Corps and Others for the Year 1860* (Washington, 1860), 16, 133. Hereafter cited as *U. S. Navy Register 1860.*
4. C. A. Vanfelson, *The Little Red Book, or Departmental Directory* (Richmond, 1861), 10. Hereafter cited as Vanfelson.
5. Navy Department General Order dated 8 July 1863, subject file VN, National Archives; *C. S. Navy Register 1864*, 87.

appropriations and with disbursing funds allocated to his department. He was spokesman for the navy in matters between executive departments. Finally, he had authority to convene general courts-martial and courts of inquiry, to reduce or commute sentences, and to order execution of sentences of less severity than dismissal of an officer. All cases calling for dismissal or death were to be referred to the president.

The Navy Department offices, except that of the Surgeon, were on the second floor of the Mechanics Institute in Richmond. The Secretary had a personal aide, a chief clerk, two to four junior clerks, and a messenger. Chief Clerk E. M. Tidball had been clerk in the United States Bureau of Ordnance and Hydrography since 1849. He was a dapper, precise, orderly man who kept good files and who never stepped beyond his position of office manager, as did men in similar positions in the United States Navy Department. He was not an assistant secretary in any respect. His signature seldom appeared on official correspondence, and he was rarely mentioned in it. Mallory needed an administrative assistant and Tidball had experience which should have been of value. Midshipman Clarence Cary, the Secretary's aide in 1863, had duties of a social character; he escorted ladies to Drewry's Bluff and read newspapers (presumably Union ones) for intelligence purposes.

The man whom Jefferson Davis appointed Secretary of the Navy on 21 March 1861 was Stephen R. Mallory of Florida. He was a logical choice; Florida as one of the first states to secede had a strong claim to a cabinet appointment and Mallory had been on the United States Senate Naval Affairs Committee for ten years, during much of that time serving as chairman. The ten years before the Civil War were years of transition of the United States Navy from sail to steam, from wood to iron, from shot to shell, from stagnation to progressivism. Mallory's part in the changes had been intimate, although neither original nor especially important.

Principal matters in which he had been interested and which he supported were reinstatement of flogging, experimental construction of the ironclad Stevens Battery, and the retirement of superannuated naval officers. Mallory developed a love for the navy and an admiration for its officers.

Mallory's appointment was not pleasing to Floridians. Mallory and a group of cautious associates had lost the Confederacy an opportunity for the easy capture of Fort Pickens in early 1861 by agreeing not to attack it if Buchanan would not reinforce it without prior notice. The use of the Pensacola Navy Yard and the best harbor on the Gulf were thus denied to the Confederacy for the entire war. However honest and excusable the mistake was, it was not forgotten; indeed, it was later denounced as treason. Mallory started his Confederate career as an unpopular man and he received little if any credit for the navy's subsequent achievements during its brief moments of glory.

If Jefferson Davis was aware of the widespread dislike of Mallory, he gave it no heed. One of the President's most prominent characteristics was his refusal to sacrifice a subordinate to public opinion. It is generally believed that Davis was satisfied or even pleased with Mallory's services as Secretary of the Navy. However, Josiah Gorgas, a close friend of Davis and an able observer, wrote in 1863 that Davis treated Mallory and the navy with open contempt, yet never controlled the Secretary in the least.[6]

Before the appointment of Mallory, Davis had taken much interest in the navy. In February 1861 he gave

6. Frank Vandiver, ed., *The Civil War Diary of Josiah Gorgas* (University, Alabama, 1947), 59.

Raphael Semmes detailed and comprehensive instructions in his own handwriting before sending him on a purchasing expedition to the North.[7] After Mallory took office, Davis gave him a freer hand than he gave the Secretaries of War. Davis personally handled the most minute matters involving army officers, but only once is he known to have interfered in naval personnel matters; in that instance he acted correctly and tactfully.[8]

President Davis' relations with the Navy Department were rather remote and formal. Perhaps one reason that Davis did not find it necessary to intervene in naval matters was the efficiency of his naval aide and nephew, John Taylor Wood. Wood, who also held a commission in the army, was a highly-respected, colorful, and thoroughly competent professional naval officer. He went on frequent inspection trips and made at least three spectacular and successful commando-type expeditions. Wood had ideal qualifications for his positions: loyalty to his principal, personal integrity, the esteem of his fellows, and a brilliant war record. After becoming aide to the President, he no longer publicly criticized Mallory.[9]

The Confederate Congress gave the Secretary everything of importance that he asked of it, but there was never a time that he had its confidence. The fall of New Orleans and the destruction of the C.S.S. *Merrimack* in the spring of 1862 marked such reversals of naval successes that they led to a sharp encounter between Mallory and Congress.[10] First a bill abolishing the Navy Department and transferring its functions to the War Department was introduced and rejected. Next a vote of censure for Mallory was proposed; this was defeated, though the vote was close, and was followed by adoption of an act providing for a joint investigation of the Navy Department.

---

7. Raphael Semmes, *Memoirs of Service Afloat* (New York, 1869), 83.
8. *O.R.N.*, ser. 1, I, 769.
9. *O.R.N.*, ser. 2, II, 256–257.
10. The Confederates knew this ship as CSS *Virginia*, but the name and spelling *Merrimack* are in such common usage that the latter will be employed in this paper.

The investigation was pointedly prejudiced and thoroughly irresponsible. Mallory declined to appear, but he did send the official documents requested, except for some which were clearly secret. He authorized Tidball and various naval officers to testify, and he was represented by counsel. The final report found Mallory blameless, but the investigation created doubts concerning the Secretary's ability and weakened public confidence in him.[11]

In interdepartmental affairs, Secretary Mallory's principal dealings were with the Treasury and War Departments. Treasury policy gave top priority to army funds, and often little remained for the navy. When the treasury tried to issue bonds as part of the payment to naval agents, Mallory protested that the navy was being used as an outlet for bonds instead of being given the money it required to pay its contractors and its agents overseas.[12] Not until the navy went directly into the carrying of cotton to Europe in Navy controlled ships did it achieve anything like financial stability, and this was generally outside the control of the Treasury Department.

With the War Department, relations were more intimate, and disagreements sharper. The persistent manpower problem will be discussed at length in Chapter 4. This problem was so great and so pervasive that it could have been solved only at the highest level. Mallory wrote several strong letters to the Secretary of War and one or two to the President, but he never went so far as to threaten to resign if the navy did not receive more equitable treatment with respect to manpower. Perhaps he was afraid that his resignation might be accepted.

Another major army-navy problem which demanded cabinet attention was river and harbor defense. Early in the war, neither Union nor Confederate strategists understood

---

11. *O.R.N.*, ser. 2, I. 431–809; *Report from the Joint Select Committee to Investigate the Navy Department* (Richmond?, 1864?), 1–7.
12. *O.R.N.*, ser, 2, I, 714–715, 736–737.

this problem and both established riverboat forces independent of naval command, but loosely under the army. On neither side did this arrangement prove satisfactory, but the worst disaster occurred to the Confederates, on the Mississippi. Riverboats were withheld from the naval commander until New Orleans was under attack and then suddenly turned over to him. Their captains ignored orders and fled the scene of battle. Mallory's subordinate and also the army commander at New Orleans had invited attention to the unworkable situation, but the central government failed to act in time.

Also involved in the river and harbor problem was the question of responsibilities for obstructions, including underwater mines. While the Norfolk Navy Yard was under navy control, there had been difficulties growing out of the navy's concern about the *Merrimack*'s ability to pass through army obstructions. After Norfolk and the *Merrimack* were lost and the Confederate naval vessels ascended the James River, both services blocked the channel. A decision was necessary and Mallory verbally approved giving the War Department complete control.[13] He lived to regret this decision when, two years later, he was unable to get the channel clear in time for the squadron to take advantage of temporary Union naval weakness near City Point.[14]

It is hard to see how the navy, with its limited manpower, could have maintained the obstructions and at the same time continued another river commitment, that of manning shore batteries. In 1861 and 1862, navy-manned shore batteries along the James, York, and Rappahannock rivers played an important part in delaying the Union advance, and it would have been foolish in the middle of the campaign against General George B. McClellan to replace the naval gun crews with soldiers who lacked their experi-

---

13. United States War Department, comp., *The War of the Rebellion: A Compilation of the Official Records of the Union and Confederate Armies* (Washington, 1880–1901), ser. 1, LI, part 2, 592. Hereafter cited as *O.R.A.*
14. *O.R.N.*, ser. 2, X, 633.

ence in handling big guns. Nevertheless, it would have been to the long-term advantage of the navy to cut its commitments on shore batteries in order to assume the responsibility for river and harbor obstructions. An alternative, to continue both functions, would have been better, but it would have required aggressive leadership by Mallory to get the size of the navy increased in order to take over more positions ashore. Mallory was not an empire builder and no Confederate naval officer, except Captain Franklin Buchanan, soon to achieve fame as the *Merrimack*'s commander, tried to get him to expand into traditional army areas of action.[15]

The relations of the Navy Department with the state governments were less complicated than those of the War Department, both because of the smaller size of the navy and because the nature of its operations forestalled collision. There were small state navies in the early days of the Confederacy, but they had few warships, few men, and were readily turned over to the central government. Local governors never tried to control operations. The Louisiana state government tried hard to prod the Navy Department into more action in defense of the mouth of the Mississippi, and cooperated to the utmost when the attack came.

Control of blockade runners was troublesome. Confederate law allowed military and naval authorities to seize a portion of all cargo spaces of the blockade runners in order to take out government cotton and to bring in necessary munitions. The state of North Carolina bought its own ship and named her the *A. D. Vance* (sometimes called *Advance* or *Ad-Vance*) after Governor Zebulon Vance. When naval authorities first preempted space and then seized coal allegedly belonging to the *A. D. Vance*, Governor Vance wrote an angry letter to Mallory, who became indignant

---

15. *O.R.N.*, series 1, VI, 733–734.

because Vance called his cruisers privateers and belittled their efforts. Mallory denounced Vance to President Davis.

Whether Mallory was truly indignant or merely wanted to tell his chief the kind of thing Davis would like to hear is a question which cannot be answered. The fact is that Mallory dearly loved the navy and delighted in the prestige of his position. A man of humble beginnings and modest talents, he seems to have attached greater importance to holding high position than to opposing the criticisms which his actions evoked.

Mallory failed to grasp the fundamentals of efficient command. He was either too abrupt and peremptory or else vague and indecisive. Early in the war, particularly in his orders to distant points like New Orleans, Mallory issued commands almost as immutable and imperative as orders to the helm. Over the protest of both army and navy commanders at New Orleans, he sent all available naval vessels upstream. When Flag Officer George N. Hollins, upriver with the gunboats, insisted that they belonged below New Orleans, Mallory refused to let them go. When Hollins left the gunboats near Memphis and hurried to New Orleans to take command of the pitifully inadequate naval force remaining there, Mallory summarily ordered him to Richmond to head a board to examine midshipmen. Mallory was clearly within his rights and possibly he was justified in his actions. Unfortunately New Orleans fell, in probably the most unexpected major disaster of the war. Mallory's self-confidence was shattered.

Meantime Mallory had been exercising exactly the opposite type of control nearer home. The orders under which first Buchanan and then Tattnall operated the *Merrimack* were vague, tentative, filled with options, and lacking in purpose. This loose control might be condoned before the ironclad had been tried, but once her characteristics and capabilities were determined in her battles with the *Cumberland, Congress,* and *Monitor* it was time for the Secretary of the Navy to make clear the policy he wanted followed. He could not make up his mind whether he wanted Norfolk protected, the Union fleet attacked, the James River blockaded, Fort Monroe run and the York River raided, or the Brooklyn Navy Yard bombarded. Tattnall, Buchanan's relief, was the kind of man who would brave the most formidable foe to carry out orders, but he would not take unnecessary chances without hope of corresponding advantage. Tattnall was critically handicapped by not knowing what was expected of him.

For the remainder of the war the Secretary's instructions to subordinates were like those to Tattnall. The usual order began with a statement that the Secretary had so much confidence in the subordinate's abilities that he would not give him explicit orders. Then followed instructions of such a general nature as to be no orders at all. The result was that subordinates usually worked in a hazy world of conjecture as to the desires of a noncommittal senior pursuing an unknown plan. Only in the romantic world of the *Alabama* or *Florida,* cruisers which were usually too distant for any real coordination, could such a system succeed.

2

The Office of Orders and Detail: General

Officers in Charge
Captain Samuel Barron: 11 June 1861–20 July 1861
Captain Lawrence L. Rousseau: about 1 August–about 23 August 1861
Captain William F. Lynch: 23 August 1861–4 September 1861
Captain Franklin Buchanan: 24 September 1861–24 February 1862
Captain French Forrest: about 27 March 1862–16 March 1863
Commander John K. Mitchell: 16 March 1863–6 May 1864
Captain S. Smith Lee: 6 May 1864–end of war

T H E Office of Orders and Detail was responsible for preparing and issuing all orders and details for service, with matters connected with courts-martial and courts of inquiry, and with such other duties relating to the personnel of the navy as the Secretary might from time to time direct.[1] The Secretary later ordered the officer in charge to assume responsibility for equipment, including outfits and stores of vessels, rope walks, and supply of fuel.[2] By virtue of his seniority among naval officers in Richmond, the officer in

---

1. W. W. Lester and Wm. J. Bromwell, comps., *A Digest of the Military and Naval Laws of the Confederate States from the Commencement of the Provisional Congress to the End of the First Congress under the Permanent Constitution* (Columbia, 1864), 200. Hereafter cited as *Digest.*
2. *O.R.N.*, ser. 2, II, 546; C. S. Navy Department General Orders, 8 June and 18 July 1863.

charge of Orders and Detail acted as the Secretary's principal adviser, assistant, and substitute, and therefore had considerably more authority than his title indicated.

The officer in charge had an officer assistant, a chief clerk, and a register whose duties will be explained in Chapter 3. Two additional clerks were added in 1864.[3]

The first officer in charge was Captain Samuel Barron, who had held a similar position in the Virginia State Navy until that organization was absorbed by the Confederate Navy. Since Barron's most important service was in Europe, he will be discussed in Chapter 17. Barron served in Richmond only about a month before being transferred to take charge of Confederate naval forces in Virginia and North Carolina. Unquestionably he had used his position near the Secretary to secure for himself an operational command. Every subsequent officer in charge except one did the same. It was natural that an officer able to do so would leave no stone unturned to secure for himself a combat command, but the Secretary should not have permitted this maneuvering.

Barron's relief was the aged and ineffective Captain Lawrence L. Rousseau of Louisiana, whose long career in the United States Navy dated from 1809. He had had only two years of sea duty since 1837 and none since the Mexican War. Rousseau was one of the naval advisers of the Confederate Congress before the war began and, until he came to Richmond, was in charge of the naval defenses of New Orleans, where his caution and reluctance to move without authority contributed to the disaster the following year.[4] Rousseau had been considered for appointment as Secretary of the Navy before Mallory was selected. Ill health seems to have been the cause of his relief from active service in

---

3. *Digest*, 200.
4. W. W. Hunter to Mallory, 15 June 1861, Hunter Collection, Tulane.

August 1861. In 1862 he served briefly on the Court of Inquiry over the destruction of the *Merrimack*.

Captain William F. Lynch was in charge only about a month when the capture of Barron at Hatteras Inlet opened a vacancy in command afloat which Lynch seized. Lynch had little or no effect on the Richmond office. Late in the war Mallory assigned him, as a writer of experience (*Narrative of the United States' Expedition to the River Jordan and the Dead Sea* [Philadelphia, 1849]), the task of preparing a history of the Confederate Navy. Lynch began collecting material in January 1865, but is unlikely to have written much before the end of the war. He died in Baltimore a few months later, and his notes have not been located.[5]

Lynch's successor as officer in charge of Orders and Detail was Captain Franklin Buchanan, an ideal man for the position, whose forty-five years in the U.S. Navy included two very important assignments in personnel management. He was the first Superintendent of the United States Naval Academy in 1845, and he had been an active member of the U.S. Navy Retiring Board in the 1850's. Buchanan showed considerable indecision about leaving the United States Navy; but, once he entered the Confederate service, he acted with more vigor and fire than did any of his contemporaries. He unquestionably owed his assignment as Officer in Charge of Orders and Detail to his work with Mallory on the Naval Retiring Board.

Buchanan, like Barron, was widely known in the navy. His appointment must have filled many officers with dismay; he was a temperance man and he expected his officers to stay sober. He hated incompetency and was intolerant of laziness. He played favorites, but his favorites were the most

---

5. *O.R.N.*, ser. 1, VII, 49.

efficient, enthusiastic officers in the Confederacy. Buchanan administered his office with efficiency and imagination. He found the army dissatisfied with the command relationships with the navy over shore batteries and offered a sensible solution. He originated little correspondence, but what he wrote was solid. The *Navy Regulations* came out during his administration, an excellent adaptation of the United States *Navy Regulations*. He went a long way toward stabilizing personnel administration, and then went a long way toward wrecking it. One after another, the outstanding lieutenants of the navy were ordered to the *Merrimack* in the winter and spring of 1861–1862. To no one's surprise, Buchanan left Richmond on 24 February 1862 to become her captain. His assignment had been predicted as early as a month after he entered the Confederate Navy.[6]

Buchanan's successor was Captain French Forrest, a veteran of fifty years service in the United States Navy. Forrest performed his duties well as commandant of the Norfolk Navy Yard for the first year of the war, although Mallory thought work on the *Merrimack* was too slow. Stung by Buchanan's criticism of his failure to participate in combat, Forrest obtained command of the James River Squadron as replacement for Captain S. Smith Lee.

Forrest's relief was Commander John K. Mitchell, who had been in command of naval forces at the fall of New Orleans. Mitchell, a younger man than his predecessors in office, was a good administrator with sensible ideas and fair grasp of the problems of his office. He was given to issuing orders to carry out orders and to demanding useless reports at inopportune times. He was seriously handicapped by a widespread belief that he had failed to do his utmost in battle. Mitchell left the Office of Orders and Detail to be-

---

6. *O.R.N.*, Ser. 1, VI, 731.

come commander of the James River Squadron, where he continued to administer rather than to fight.

His successor was Captain Sidney Smith Lee, elder brother of General Robert E. Lee and father of General Fitzhugh Lee. Smith Lee's forty years naval service had included command of Commodore Matthew C. Perry's flagship U.S.S. *Mississippi* on the first cruise to Japan and command of the Coastal Survey. He was considered even more handsome and gallant than his younger brother. He and his wife both opposed secession; Mrs. Lee, a member of the Mason family, said that she had been dragged across the Long Bridge from Washington kicking.[7] Smith Lee had an unrewarding but praiseworthy Confederate career as commandant of the Norfolk Navy Yard, of the James River Squadron, and of the naval batteries at Drewry's Bluff. By the time he became officer in charge of Orders and Detail it was too late for the navy to benefit from any changes he might have made, although his direct and informal ways must have been a relief after Mitchell's avalanche of paper work.

Lee, Barron, or Buchanan would probably have been an effective officer in charge had any of them been kept in the position for two or more years, but their full capabilities could not be realized in the few months they served.

---

7. Ben Ames Williams, ed., *A Diary from Dixie* (Boston, 1949) 94, 104.

3

The Office of Orders and Detail: Personnel

THE establishment of the Office of Orders and Detail in the Confederate Navy was an improvement over the United States Navy practice of handling personnel matters in the office of the Secretary. Nevertheless the Secretary continued to be more closely involved in personnel problems than he was in any other portion of his department. This was especially true of the assignment and performance of officers.

Officers were classified into three major categories: commissioned, warrant, and appointed. Commissioned officers included all those nominated by the President and subject to approval by the senate. Warrant officers received their status from the Secretary of the Navy. Appointed officers owed their ranks to a senior officer who had specific authorization from the Secretary to make their appointments.[1]

Commissioned officers eligible for command afloat were called sea or line officers. They considered themselves the elite corps of the navy. Some warrant officers were also eligible for general command positions. The remaining officers succeeded to command only within their own corps, unless specially designated.[2]

---

1. *Regulations of the Navy of the Confederate States* (Richmond, 1862), 6. Hereafter cited as *C. S. Navy Regulations.*
2. Confederate States Navy Department, comp., *Register of the Commissioned and Warrant Officers of the Navy of the Confederate States, to January 1, 1863* (Richmond, 1862), 1. Hereafter cited as *C. S. Navy Register 1863.*

Ranks of commissioned sea officers in descending order were admiral, vice admiral, rear admiral, captain, commander, lieutenant (changed to first and second lieutenant by act of the Confederate congress in 1862), and lieutenant for the war. The rank of flag officer was a temporary rank awarded to a captain assigned command of a squadron.[3] Master, passed midshipman, midshipman, boatswain, gunner, and master's mate were warranted sea officers. Surgeon, paymaster, chief engineer, naval constructor, passed assistant surgeon, assistant paymaster, and assistant surgeon were also commissioned but not sea officers. First, second, and third assistant engineer, carpenter, and sailmaker were warrant officers not of the sea officer group. Appointed officers included secretary to a flag officer, clerk to a captain, and clerk to a paymaster. Chaplains were included in the pay scales and uniform regulations and their duties were outlined in Confederate *Navy Regulations*, but none is known to have been appointed.

The maximum number of naval officers on active duty at one time (April 1864) was 727, with twenty-six others on sick leave, awaiting orders, or suspended.[4]

There was much question as to the equivalent ranks in army and navy. By act of 16 February 1864, these were fixed as follows: admirals ranked with generals, rear admirals with major generals, flag officers with brigadier generals, captains with colonels, commanders with lieutenant colonels, first lieutenants with majors, second lieutenants with captains, lieutenants for the war with chaplains, and masters and passed midshipmen with lieutenants. The relative ranks of other officers depended upon their length of service.[5]

The initial legislation of 16 March 1861 set a modest limit on the number of officers to be appointed: four cap-

---

3. *U. S. Navy Register 1860*, 143.
4. *O.R.N.*, ser. 2, II, 640.
5. *C. S. Navy Register 1864*, 80.

tains, four commanders, thirty lieutenants, five surgeons, five assistant surgeons, six paymasters, two chief engineers, and as many other officers as the president deemed necessary.[6] The law did not so provide, but it was clear that only officers who had resigned as a consequence of secession were expected to be appointed. In May congress authorized the appointment of all such officers at their old ranks.[7] By August 1861 the Confederacy had thirty five captains and commanders and only a few improvised warships and very modest plans for expansion. Thus the navy began its existence badly overranked for its size. Most problems concerning officers stemmed from this fact.

There were adequate numbers of lieutenants, surgeons, paymasters, and chief engineers, but the warrant officers, except for inexperienced and immature midshipmen, were in short supply. In December 1861, congress authorized the appointment of additional officers from civil life, but no qualifications or means of procurement were established.[8]

The promotion system of the United States Navy was carried over without change. Promotion was allowed only to fill vacancies and vacancies occurred only through death, resignation, or dismissal. Only one set of examinations was given, that to establish eligibility for promotion to lieutenant, chief engineer, surgeon, or acting paymaster. It had been usual for United States Navy officers to pass the examination one or more years before they were likely to be promoted and then wait for an opening to occur. The procedures in the medical, supply, and engineering branches are discussed in Chapters 12, 13, and 15. Since the naval school was assigned to the Office of Ordnance and Hydrography, the sea officers examination will be discussed in Chapter 11, even though it was held under the auspices of Orders and Detail.

---

6. *Digest*, 202.
7. *Ibid.*, 209.
8. *Ibid.*, 210.

The Office of Orders and Detail established the officer complement of each ship and was responsible for keeping it filled with appropriately trained men. Assignments were recommended to the Secretary by the officer in charge from a list of officers kept by a clerk known as the register. The register (John C. Jones for most of the war) was required to record name, rank, date of rank, time in service, sea duty in rank, name of state in which born, from which appointed, and of which a citizen. It was customary for officers of the rank of captain unassigned or on shore duty to be offered commands afloat in order of their seniority, but this was not obligatory. Lesser officers who were awaiting assignment were either asked for by a commanding officer or assigned by the office from the register in order of seniority.

The register also was required to keep a file on each unassigned officer which included appropriate correspondence such as his application for service, his reasons for declining a given service, the reason he returned from overseas before the end of his cruise, charges preferred or complaints lodged against him with their dispositions, and his reasons for leaving a previous service.[9]

In some cases senior army officers asked for a naval officer by name or qualification. Officers selected for army duty were ordered to report to the Secretary of War. The Adjutant General's office then issued a special order assigning them duty stations. In December 1861, President Davis was authorized to assign temporary military rank and command to navy officers serving with troops.[10] A number of officers including J. Taylor Wood, Richard L. Page, and Raphael Semmes held and utilized such rank. In view of the great shortage of experienced officers in the rapidly expanding army and the great excess of naval officers for a

---

9. *C. S. Navy Regulations,* 152.
10. *C. S. Navy Register 1864,* 72.

slowly growing navy, it was unfortunate that so few men chose to make the transfer.

Sailors in the Confederate Navy fell into two main categories: petty officers and seamen. The petty officer rating was a temporary one, fairly easily won and quite easily lost. The petty officers in descending order of rank were as follows:

The grade of master's mate, not warranted, lasted not less than a year, at the end of which time a warrant might be issued by the Secretary of the Navy. There were few master's mates at the beginning of the war, but the rate became increasingly common. The master's mate was essentially an officer candidate in the seamanship branch of the navy.[11]

The master at arms, chief police officer of the ship, oversaw the internal discipline of the ship in such matters as making prisoners secure, ensuring that lights were turned out, and smoking regulations observed.

The yeoman was responsible for storage, inventory, and issue of ship's stores and provisions.

The schoolmaster appeared on the list of authorized personnel but no record has been found of the appointment of petty officers in this rate. Instructors at the Naval School were either officers or civilians.

The surgeon's steward was an assistant to the medical officer and was expected to know something of pharmacy.

The ship's corporal was an assistant to the master at arms.

The armorer was responsible for maintenance of small arms, cutlasses, pikes, and other weapons for hand-to-hand fighting.

The cooper was manufacturer and repairman of casks, barrels, pumps, and similar bulk containers.

---

11. *C. S. Navy Register 1864*, 90, 91.

The ship's cook prepared bread, meat, and some desserts for the crew.

The boatswain's mate handled the deck rigging and seamanship.

The gunner's mate maintained guns and ammunition.

The carpenter's mate made and repaired wooden parts of the ship. An important duty was to take soundings of the holds and storerooms to detect leakage of water.

The sailmaker's mate was responsible for canvas throughout the ship.

The coxswain to the squadron commander was in charge of the flag officer's boat.

The quartermaster was assistant to the master and his master's mates. He steered the ship, took depth soundings, and assisted in navigation generally.

The quarter gunner was a subordinate of the gunner's mate.

The coxswain was in charge of a boat.

Captains of the forecastle, maintop, foretop, after guard, hold, and mizzen top were experienced salts who looked to the rigging or storerooms in their parts of the ship. They were assigned to the master's division, whereas the boatswain's mates were in the gun divisions.

A fireman first class was the only engineering department petty officer. He was expected to be able to run the engines without supervision, although regulations required an engineer officer, if available, to be on watch at all times.

The painter was responsible for mixing and issuing paint.

The master of the band was another rating not found to be filled.

The steward to the commanding officer of a squadron was attached to the flag officer's staff and served meals, cleaned the cabin, and looked after his principal's uniform. He was often a foreigner.

The armorer's mate assisted the armorer.

The cabin steward and wardroom steward looked after the commanding officer and wardroom officers in the same manner as the steward to a commanding officer of a squadron served his superior, but with less elegance.

The cabin cook prepared meals for the captain or squadron commander. The wardroom cook prepared meals for the lesser officers.

Only master's mates, boatswain's mates, gunner's mates, coxswains, quartermaster, quarter gunners, and captains of tops and holds succeeded to military command.

Men below petty officer status, generally called seamen regardless of their actual pay grade, were seaman, ordinary seaman, landsman, fireman second class, coal heaver, and boy. Most of the titles were the same as those used by the merchant marine, from which navies traditionally drew their sailors. A man going to sea for the first time shipped as a landsman or a coal heaver and worked his way up. Youngsters between the ages of fourteen and about seventeen were shipped as boys, their status depending upon strength and maturity rather than age.

The traditional way to ship men was to establish a rendezvous in a seaport city under the charge of a relatively senior, often partially disabled, sea officer with a surgeon and two or three junior officers to assist him. Advertisements were inserted in the newspapers and announcements were posted in prominent places. Rendezvous were established at New Orleans, Savannah, Mobile, Raleigh, Norfolk, Macon, and Richmond. The recruiting officer was supposed to interview each man and determine at what pay grade the navy would ship him. Even a man who had served many years as a petty officer could officially reenter the navy at no higher status than seaman unless specific authorization was received from the Navy Department.[12]

In order to enter the navy a man had to be at least fourteen years old and four feet eight inches tall. If he was less than twenty-one, he had to have parental consent. If he was a free man of color, special permission from the Navy Department or the local squadron commander had to be received. Slaves could be enlisted with their owners' approval; there is no way to tell how many slaves served, but there are occasional references to such service, particularly as pilots, firemen, and officers' servants. A landsman could be no older than twenty-five unless he had a special and useful trade, in which case the maximum age was thirty-five. Ordinary seamen were required to have completed at least a year's sea duty and seamen must have had two years.

The medical officer was directed to examine each applicant and to certify his general fitness for duty. Physically handicapped persons possessed of special qualifications could be accepted on the recommendation of the recruiting and the medical officer, but the reason for waiver had to be noted on the shipping articles and signed by both officers.[13]

The recruiting officer was supplied with printed shipping articles which he was not allowed to modify. Intoxicated men could not be shipped and bounty was not to be offered without permission of the Secretary of the Navy. The rendezvous transferred men to receiving ships designated by the Office of Orders and Detail and made a weekly report of men enlisted to that office.[14] Men received from conscript camps or from drafts on the army were treated as if coming through a rendezvous.

Receiving ships were obsolete men of war or over-age merchantmen permanently stationed in a major seaport.

---

12. *U. S. Navy Regulations*, 162.
13. *C. S. Navy Regulations*, 163.
14. *Ibid.*, 166.

They were in full commission and generally fully rigged so that training exercises could be held on board. When a draft of men was received from a rendezvous, each man was entered on a descriptive list containing his name, the rendezvous through which he entered, period of enlistment, age, place of birth, complexion, height, color, rating, trade, and marks and scars. Copies were sent to the Secretary of the Navy on 1 July and 1 January. The descriptive list, to which were added special qualifications and record of service as a petty officer, accompanied a man from ship to ship. Entries were signed by the captain of the ship and the paymaster.

The receiving ship was responsible for a man's indoctrination. His clothing was inventoried, marked, and inspected, and he was required to purchase articles to fill deficiencies, the cost being borne by his pay account, which included an allowance for clothing. The recruit received such training as the receiving ship could offer, including instruction in exercising at great and small guns, reefing and furling sails, and pulling boats. Men at receiving ships were not given liberty without permission of the station commander.[15]

When a new ship was to be placed into commission, the station commandant made up a list specifying the number of men of each rating that he thought should be attached. The Office of Orders and Detail reviewed, corrected, and approved the list and ordered the station commandant to detail the men from his receiving ship. The complement included petty officers as well as non-rated men, but no one was transferred as a petty officer. The receiving ship commander determined qualifications from descriptive lists and ordered to the ship men who could be promoted by the new captain to fill the billets of petty officers. Each outgoing draft was supposed to be a fair sample of men available to the re-

15. *Ibid.,* 173.

ceiving ship, but not more than one-twentieth of a draft was to be Negroes, without the specific authorization of the commanding officer of the station. Officers not attached to the receiving ship were forbidden to choose their men, but men could request a particular assignment and commanding officers of ships frequently asked for specific men with whom they had served.

When vacancies appeared on a ship already in commission, the captain requested replacement through his squadron commander, who sent consolidated lists to the commanding officer of the station. He ordered the receiving ship to send replacements if available; otherwise he reported to the Office of Orders and Detail, who ordered a station having sailors to send a draft. Commanding officers were required to notify the Office of Orders and Detail of the number of petty officers and men of each grade, noting deficiencies or excess. In addition, a copy of the complete muster roll was required in Richmond on the first of January, first of July, and before sailing.[16] When groups of twenty or more men were being transferred, they had to be in charge of a lieutenant or a master.[17]

When a man's enlistment expired, he was to be discharged within the Confederate States. If he had served with fidelity and obedience, he could be recommended for an honorable discharge which would entitle him to three months extra pay upon reenlistment.[18] If he were disabled in action, he was entitled to half pay; after 17 February 1864, he was given full pay but required to enroll in the Invalid Corps, if physically able to perform even limited duties.[19]

16. *Ibid.*, 53, 82.
17. *Ibid.*, 21.
18. *C. S. Navy Register 1864*, 70.
19. *Ibid.*, 81.

4

The Office of Orders and Detail:
Operation of the System

THE personnel management system was essentially the one which had been developed during about fifty years of United States Navy operations. Suited to a peacetime organization, it had a number of weaknesses which vigorous and imaginative handling could correct. This section will consider some of the problems and attempts toward solutions, and will evaluate the performance of the Confederate Navy with respect to personnel.

The most annoying problem concerning officers, as previously noted, was a surplus of senior officers. When the secession process had been completed, the Confederate Navy included more than a hundred officers eligible for command afloat who had naval service of ten to fifty years to their credit. Of these, ten were captains, twenty-five were commanders, and about seventy were lieutenants. Many were outstanding officers of whom any service at any time would have been proud. Some were hopelessly incompetent, and these could have been thrust aside without serious criticism. The problem lay with those officers who had achieved fame and prestige but because of advancing age or limited outlook showed no promise for the future. Although some of this group had strong local political backing, their professionalism prevented this from being the serious problem that it was in the army. Promotion by seniority resulted in further stagnation.

The situation was an aggravated version of the problem Mallory had faced with his Navy Retiring Board in 1853. Even some of the officers were the same. A solution which Mallory never attempted lay in restricting the number of officers in each grade to those currently needed. An alternative used by Union Secretary of Navy Gideon Welles was to keep the unfit out of the way by leaving them unassigned or by giving them unimportant jobs.

First Mallory tried a positive approach; soon after Franklin Buchanan became officer in charge of Orders and Detail, an act was passed which permitted two captains, five commanders, fifty lieutenants, and a number of other officers to be given temporary appointments to these grades either from the navy or from civil life, without regard to previous service or seniority.[1]

A law passed 16 March 1862 allowed the appointment of four admirals, divided the rank of lieutenant into the grades of first and second lieutenant, and reserved some of these positions as rewards for gallant or meritorious service.[2]

Hardly had this act been passed when Mallory nullified it by appointing as officer in charge of Orders and Detail Captain French Forrest, such a thorough-going believer in promotion by seniority that Buchanan's promotion to admiral over his head made him ill. He began to lobby for repeal of the meritorious promotion law.[3] His efforts were fruitless, but as late as May 1864 some naval officers were trying to persuade Congress to restore promotion by seniority.[4]

One administrative step taken by Mallory in April

---

1. *C. S. Navy Register 1864*, 73.
2. *Ibid.*
3. *O.R.N.*, ser. 2, II, 256.
4. *Ibid.*, 648.

1863 to place tactical command in the hands of young and presumably vigorous officers was to require commanders of naval stations to transfer command of forces afloat in their areas to officers designated by the Navy Department.[5] Thereafter, commanding officers of naval stations, who comprised almost all of the oldest officers in the service, were responsible only for logistic support and administrative matters. Since these orders were issued soon after Commander John K. Mitchell became officer in charge of Orders and Detail, they were probably the result of Mitchell's bitter experience in New Orleans in April 1862 when he suddenly found himself in an improvised command afloat only a few days before he had to defend the Mississippi against the assault of the forty-three-ship Union fleet under Flag Officer David G. Farragut. The orders were also issued only a week after French Forrest left the office, and it is possible Forrest had resisted their issuance earlier.

Mallory's orders assigning command afloat to officers under his personal direction involved only units in Georgia, South Carolina, and North Carolina. Command of the James River Squadron had already been divorced from that of shore commanders during the peninsula campaign in the spring of 1862. The command in Alabama under Franklin Buchanan continued to include both elements. The administrative step thus taken left on active service senior officers whom Mallory considered ineffective, and it neither brought about any marked increase in activity afloat nor opened vacancies for promotion.

Mallory, still dissatisfied with the composition of the officer corps, obtained legislation which he hoped would improve it. On 1 May 1863, congress established the provisional navy. All naval personnel fit for service except commissioned officers were incorporated into it, and the

---

5. Josiah Tattnall to S. R. Mallory, 24 April 1863 in C. S. Jones, *The Life and Services of Josiah Tattnall* (Savannah, 1878), 221–226.

President was empowered to appoint, subject to senatorial confirmation, such officers as he deemed necessary. Officers could be appointed from civil life or from the regular navy, but regular navy officers of each rank took precedence over non-regulars. Regular navy officers assumed the same seniority within their provisional navy grades as they had held in the regular navy list. There was no limitation on the number of officers in each grade.[6]

In the first year of its existence, the provisional navy contained only nine commissioned officers, all appointed one grade above their regular navy ranks or commissioned from civil life. No major command was affected, and no appreciable change in spirit or performance resulted.

On 2 June 1864 virtually every officer in the regular navy except a number of captains and commanders was assigned to the provisional navy. Of the eight captains and twenty commanders not so assigned, all except four captains and four commanders (most of whom were ill) remained on active service ashore or abroad. Officers not in the provisional navy but still on important duty in late 1864 included the officers in charge of all the administrative offices in Richmond, the commander at Drewry's Bluff, the representatives in Europe, and commanders of all the important industrial establishments. The provisional navy included all the officers serving afloat.[7] Raphael Semmes is inaccurate when he states that the regular navy was made a kind of retired list by the adoption of a provisional navy.[8]

By October 1864, the officer in charge of Orders and Detail recommended transfer of all officers to the provisional navy, since the maintenance of two lists was an impediment to prompt assignment of officers from shore to sea duty. The device had served a useful purpose in allowing promotion of a few enterprising officers over the heads of

---

6. *C. S. Navy Register 1864*, 78–79.
7. *Ibid.*, 4–31.
8. Semmes, 368–369.

ineffective seniors, but it had not brought about the reform of the officer corps for which it had been devised. The assignment of officers to whatever duty the secretary considered appropriate had always been within his authority and needed only to be exercised with imagination and firmness to have achieved the ends the secretary desired.

While there were too many senior officers, there were too few junior officers, particularly after the midshipmen were withdrawn from the fleet and sent to the naval school. The gap left by the midshipmen was filled by master's mates, a rank which had disappeared from the United States Navy as early as 1847 because it was expected that all future sea officers would be trained at the naval academy.[9] War forced both sides into resurrecting the grade in order to meet promptly the enormous demand for junior officers. To receive an appointment by the Confederate Secretary of the Navy, a man had to be over twenty years old, to pass an examination in seamanship, mathematics, and navigation, to pass a physical examination, and to produce references as to his good character.[10]

The system produced a large number of officers; the *Navy Register* for 1864 listed ninety-six acting master's mates. Some of the appointees had been merchant officers or pilots, some had been sailors in the navy, and others were from the army or civil life. They were not uniformly effective, and desertions were more frequent among them than among any of the other officers. A circular from the Office of Orders and Detail in March 1864 enjoined examining boards not to recommend for appointment as master's mate any candidate who did not possess adequate practical knowledge for the position.[11] In September the office directed commanders to report the names of those who did not come

---

9. *U. S. Navy Register 1860,* 150.
10. *C. S. Navy Regulations,* 27.
11. *C. S. Navy Register 1864,* 90.

up to standard so that they could be discharged and conscripted into the army.[12]

In connection with sailors, the most serious problem was getting a sufficient number. It was soon apparent that usual recruiting methods were inadequate. A bounty of fifty dollars was offered in January 1862 by the Secretary for anyone enlisting for three years or the war, and the recruiting officer at New Orleans gave two dollars for his trouble to anyone who brought in a recruit.[13] The first conscription act, passed 16 April 1862, allowed seamen and ordinary seamen who had been conscripted and who requested naval service to be transferred to the navy upon application for them by the Secretary of the Navy.[14] Although the Secretary repeatedly requested transfers under this act, he got few sailors. When Lieutenant Isaac Brown, about to complete the *Arkansas*, asked for men, he received only six of twenty-five soldiers who volunteered for the Navy. He sought assistance from President Davis. Instead of ordering the Secretary of War to release men, Davis asked the governor of Mississippi to help obtain recruits.[15] The *Arkansas* fought her brilliant action near Vicksburg short-handed and with some army troops temporarily assigned.

As the navy shipbuilding and conversion program got underway in the fall of 1862, the shortage of sailors became acute. Perceiving this, the Union Secretary of the Navy aggravated the situation by refusing or delaying the exchange of sailors and pilots taken prisoner.[16]

Still, the Confederate Secretary of the Navy allowed himself to be put off with promises of cooperation by the Secretary of War.[17] When congress established conscript camps in October 1862 with provision for seafaring men to be assigned to the navy on their own application, War De-

---

12. W. W. Hunter to S. S. Lee, 21 September 1864, Hunter Collection, Tulane University.
13. *C. S. Navy Register 1864*, 73; *O.R.N.*, ser. 2, I, 464.
14. *O.R.A.*, ser. 4, I, 1095–1097.
15. *O.R.N.*, ser. 1, XIX, 70–74.
16. *O.R.A.*, ser. 2, IV, 346.
17. *Ibid.*, ser. 4, II, 90.

partment instructions placed responsibility on army officers to make the selections. These officers refused to consider as seafarers men with experience on riverboats or harbor craft and the navy got few men. Laws in May 1863 and February 1864 were likewise nullified by administrative action. Nothing has been found to indicate that Mallory did more than remonstrate mildly with the Secretary of War and the President.[18]

At last, on 22 March 1864, after a general conscription law was passed, the Adjutant General directed the major army commanders to release a total of 1,200 men to the navy.[19] Commanders of naval stations sent teams consisting of a lieutenant and a doctor to enrollment camps, and they conducted a total of 960 men, many of them experienced sailors, to their stations.[20]

The navy had a brush with the courts in July 1863 over the case of the crew of the ironclad *Georgia* in the Savannah River. The crew consisted mostly of a military company which volunteered to transfer to the navy for a year's duty beginning on 4 July 1862. On 2 April 1863, an act of congress extended to three years or the war any enlistment due to expire before the cessation of hostilities. About seventy-seven of the *Georgia*'s men applied for discharge and were refused. Some of them got writs of habeas corpus, requiring the navy to discharge them to the courts. Several times the commander of forces afloat at Savannah asked help of the Secretary of the Navy but he received none. The men were ordered discharged on 23 July 1863.[21]

The cruisers had comparatively little trouble recruiting; they followed merchant marine practice of paying wages high enough to induce men to ship, and by special permission of Secretary Mallory they paid in gold. It was not unusual for the *Alabama* or the *Shenandoah* to enlist

---

18. Stephen R. Mallory Diary, 1 August 1862.
19. *O.R.N.*, ser. 1, XV, 222, 725; XXI, 889; *O.R.A.*, ser. 4, III, 491.
20. *O.R.N.*, ser. 1, XV, 678, 725; ser. 2, II, 754.
21. *Ibid.*, ser. 1, XIV, 714–733 passim.

men from captured vessels. Nearly all the men on these cruisers were foreigners.[22]

The difficulties in recruiting and retaining men (for desertion was as common in the navy as it was in the army) might not have been so serious but for the erratic transfer policy. Shortages of men and threats of attacks at various points along coasts and rivers caused a constant shift of Confederate sailors from port to port. Army units transferred from one command to another generally brought their familiar equipment with them; but no two ships were alike, having heavy guns of various characteristics and engines of all sorts of origins. Each time sailors were transferred, they had to be trained almost as if they had never been embarked before. Time after time commanders protested transfers, but the practice continued to the end of the war.

Furthermore, Mallory and John Taylor Wood loved the drama and excitement of raids: amphibious attacks, boarding parties, and schemes to free prisoners of war. The raids were usually well planned and well executed, but they were not important to the war and each required fifteen to 150 trained men for periods up to a month. Only from the ships could the necessary officers and men be obtained.

Often confused with the provisional navy but having no relation to it was the volunteer navy. The latter was intended to make privateering palatable to foreign countries by controlling the men engaged in that pursuit. The owner of a ship of over one hundred tons capacity might register his vessel, officers, and crew with the Confederate Navy. If the officers and men were acceptable morally and physically, they could be appointed or shipped into the volunteer navy. Pay, only allowed while on sea duty, amounted to about ten per cent of regular or provisional navy pay. The volunteers were allowed to capture, burn, or destroy enemy mer-

---

22. Ella Lonn, *Foreigners in the Confederacy* (Chapel Hill, 1940), 297.

chant vessels in privateer fashion, but were required to turn over to the Confederacy ten per cent of the value of the capture.[23] The law authorizing the volunteer navy went into effect in April 1863 but was used little if at all.

The Office of Orders and Detail was also concerned with problems relating to civilians in navy employ even though it had no specific assignment to handle such problems. Workers called strikes to raise wages. Strikes cost not only money which the government could print copiously but also time of which it was short.

The military status of workers was a source of controversy from the beginning. In Norfolk this situation was partially relieved by the formation of companies composed entirely of workers under the command of the Navy Yard marine officer. At New Orleans it became necessary for the constructors to go to the highest military authority to secure temporary exemption of their artisans to complete the ironclads.

In all parts of the Confederacy, so many workers were called up with their companies or by conscription that industrial production was seriously impaired. Military necessity and public opinion demanded that a minimum number of men be exempt from military duty. The navy's civilian manpower problem was only part of a national dilemma, but it was more serious for the navy than it was for the army or civilians. The building of steam-driven ironclads was largely an industrial problem. Production of food and fiber involved work which could be accomplished by unskilled women, slaves, or invalids; even the manufacture of small arms and gunpowder did not demand the technical skills and physical strength that were required for making steam engines, heavy guns, projectiles, and armor.

---

23. *C. S. Navy Register 1864,* 75–77.

Several expedients were tried to relieve the manpower shortage. Even before the war started Raphael Semmes was sent North to recruit artisans to make fuses and primers. European representatives contracted for men to operate forges, to set up steel mills, or to manufacture steel-nosed projectiles, offering such inducements as payment in gold and extra rations. A number of Europeans were brought in through the blockade; others were captured attempting to enter the Confederacy. The employment of Europeans was not successful for several reasons: many found wartime living conditions too stringent; their high pay caused unrest among their fellow workers who were Confederate citizens; pressure was brought on them to enter the army or at least to enroll in the militia.

The wage scale was one source of much trouble. Workmen were sometimes offered higher wages by the navy than the law permitted the War Department to pay.[24] The War Department complained of labor piracy, and an army-navy agreement was arranged whereby neither would hire a workman who had not been formally released by the other. This agreement extended to civilian firms who had contracts with either service.[25]

The army, by virtue of its control of the Bureau of Conscription, enjoyed an enormous advantage over the navy. Early in the war, it was possible for industrial establishments to secure deferments or exemptions for workers, but by February 1864 all able-bodied white men between seventeen and fifty were conscripted. Enrolling officers were directed to cease respecting certificates of exemption issued by the Secretary of the Navy, and thenceforth the Secretary had to request details of soldiers to do navy work.[26] It then became necessary to ask for soldiers to be detailed for work

---

24. Frank Vandiver, ed., *The Civil War Diary of Josiah Gorgas* (University, Alabama, 1947), 166–167, 212–213.
25. *C. S. Navy Register 1864*, 88.
26. *O.R.A.*, ser. 4, III, 305.

as a military duty. Their wages were set by law at their regular pay plus stated amounts as incentive pay. Details had to be renewed every two months.[27] Not only was it difficult to get and keep a man; it was also a tremendous administrative load to maintain the records required by the Bureau and to prevent desertion by detailed men or civilian workers.[28]

Commanders of naval industrial plants felt that the government's attitude towards their workers was unrealistic and short-sighted. For instance, the commandant of the Naval Ordnance Works at Selma, in renewing a request for about seventy ironworkers, stated:

> Had my application for [about sixty-five additional] mechanics been granted the rolling-mill would have been in operation last fall and it would have rolled iron enough for all our vessels, and we would also have cast guns for all their batteries and furnished them to the fortifications. The rolling-mill is not yet in operation. We cannot turn out more than one gun a week, but with a proper number of mechanics could turn out three a week, and in a few months one a day. We have not been able to furnish shot and shell for the guns we have made. We ought to supply the whole navy.[29]

In August 1864 the total number of men detailed to the navy amounted to only 451 men of conscript age.[30] At last, in December 1864, a bill was introduced in congress to transfer all detailed men working for naval installations to the navy.[31] In February 1865 Mallory reported that 1,082 white men and 1,143 Negroes were required by his department.[32] It is not known whether or not the men were transferred to the navy; at that time five hundred sixty-one soldiers were still detailed to the navy.[33]

The administration of Confederate naval personnel

---

27. *C. S. Navy Register 1864*, 89; *O.R.A.*, ser. 4, III, 493.
28. *C. S. Navy Register 1864*, 87, 89; *O.R.A.*, ser. 4, III, 520–523.
29. *Ibid.*, ser. 4, III, 523.
30. *Ibid.*, ser. 4, III, 872.
31. H. R. 279, Emory Special Collections.
32. Message from the President, 7 February 1865, Emory Special Collections.
33. *O.R.A.*, ser. 4, III. 1.

was far below the standard which it was possible to achieve. No satisfactory solution to the problem of topheavy officer rank structure was ever put into practice. The system of procurement and training of engineers, master's mates, and pilots was inadequate and unrealistic. The Confederacy ended the war with the same difficulties in officer personnel that it had at the start.

There were not enough sailors. The maximum enlisted strength was 4,460, at least twenty-five per cent below requirements.[34] For too much of the war, even after conscription began, the navy depended upon peacetime methods of recruiting trained seamen. The Navy Department does not seem to have realized until quite late that there were not enough trained mariners to fill its needs through voluntary enlistments, and therefore the Department was slow in demanding its share of conscripts. When the army refused to transfer the modest number of men requested by the navy, it was time for the Secretary of the Navy to go to the President for support and to have resigned if he did not get it.

The short-sighted system of robbing Peter to pay Paul was disastrous to the navy. No ship could have operated properly under the difficulties experienced by most Confederate vessels. In some cases, every man was taken off a ship in order to make a foray against an isolated enemy outpost or ship. If the ships had been up to or over complement, small detachments might possibly have been sent out for short periods of time, but a short-handed ship cannot afford the luxury of landing parties.

In passing judgment on the navy's failure to cope with the problems of civilian personnel, cognizance must be taken of the Confederacy's inadequate resources and its lack

---

34. *O.R.N.*, ser. 2, II, 640.

of experience in industrial enterprise. The navy could not wholly ignore public opinion, and public opinion in the Confederacy was clearly against having a large industrial force when there was a scarcity of soldiers on the fighting fronts.

5

The Office of Orders and Detail: Legal System

THE Confederate Navy used the same legal system that had been in effect in the United States Navy since 1800 and would remain in use practically unchanged until 1950. In addition to *Navy Regulations*, the basic document was entitled "An act for the better government of the United States Navy." A modification forbidding flogging and a supplementary "Act to provide a more efficient discipline for the Navy" completed the framework of legal procedure with which the Confederate Navy worked.[1]

Three procedural bodies were provided: a court of inquiry, a general court-martial, and a summary court-martial.

The court of inquiry was a fact-finding group appointed by the President, Secretary of the Navy, or the commander of a fleet or squadron. It consisted of three commissioned officers and a judge advocate. It could summon witnesses, administer oaths, or punish contempt in the same manner as courts-martial. A court of inquiry was generally limited to ascertaining fact, but might be asked for opinion. It could not award punishment except for contempt.[2]

A general court-martial, composed of five to thirteen commissioned officers, could be ordered by the President,

---

1. *C. S. Navy Register 1864*, 63–71.
2. *C. S. Navy Register 1864*, 68.

the Secretary of the Navy, the commander-in-chief of a fleet or a squadron commander on foreign service. This body could prescribe any usual punishment including execution, but the latter sentence required concurrence of two-thirds of the members present and approval by the President except when the trial took place abroad, in which event approval could be given by a fleet or squadron commander. Other sentences except dismissal of an officer were determined by majority vote and were put into execution by the commander of the fleet or the officer ordering the court. Dismissals required presidential approval.[3]

The summary court-martial could be ordered upon petty officers and persons of inferior ratings by the commander of any warship. It consisted of three officers not below the rank of passed midshipman and a competent person (not necessarily an officer) designated as recorder. The recorder acted in a similar manner to the judge advocate of a general court-martial. Trial was considerably less formal, but evidence had to be recorded and, as in a general court-martial, the record of proceedings and evidence had to be forwarded to the Navy Department. A summary court-martial could order a bad conduct discharge (not to be executed abroad), solitary confinement in single or double irons, on bread and water, and diminished or full rations not exceeding thirty days. It could order confinement for up to two months, reduction to the next inferior rating, or deprivation of liberty on foreign shore. It could assign extra police duties and loss of pay for a period of up to three months. Approval of the officer ordering the court was required before the sentence was placed into effect. A medical officer was required to report any injury to the prisoner's health which the sentence might incur.[4]

A quarterly return of punishments, required by navy

3. *Ibid.*, 66–68.
4. *Ibid.*, 70–71.

regulations, included name of the prisoner, rating, offense, punishment, remarks if any, and signature of the commanding officer.[5]

Confederate naval courts, particularly in cases involving senior officers, used an inordinate amount of time, manpower, and effort. The trial of Josiah Tattnall for destroying the *Merrimack*, for instance, required the presence of many important officers for three weeks. The same is true of the trial of John K. Mitchell following the battle of New Orleans. The trials of such officers for questions of judgment were not to the interest of the Confederacy. Mallory would have been better advised to have followed the example of his adversary Gideon Welles in such cases and used arbitrary administrative means to punish or render harmless officers whose conduct he disapproved.

---

5. *C. S. Navy Regulations*, 235.

6

The Office of Orders and Detail:
Materiel Responsibilities

T H E original Navy Department organization gave no ma-
teriel responsibilities to the Office of Orders and Detail,
but it quickly fell heir to a number of the functions fulfilled by the United States Navy's Bureau of Construction,
Equipment, and Repair. The reorganizations of the Confederate Navy Department in June and July 1863 gave the
office, in addition to the personnel and command functions
already discussed, cognizance over supplies of coal, and the
equipment of vessels except the ordnance.

The ropewalk at Petersburg, Virginia, the only industrial establishment managed by the Office of Orders and
Detail, began production about 1 January 1863 and produced enough cotton rope, tarred cotton (substitute for
marlin or tarred hemp needed for standing rigging on sailing vessels), and other cordage to supply the needs of the
army and navy and still have some available to sell to civilians for use in coal mines, railroads, and canal companies.
During its eighteen months of operation for the government, the factory made a profit.[1]

Obtaining coal was difficult throughout the existence
of the Confederacy. The principal mines were near Rich-

---

1. *O.R.N.*, ser. 2, II, 754–755.

mond, Chattanooga, and Montevallo, Alabama, and the Egypt mines in North Carolina. Anthracite was obtainable only through capture.

In the early days, both Ordnance and Hydrography and Provisions and Clothing made contracts for coal and reported to the Secretary. Naval agents or special coal agents under the Office of Provisions and Clothing obtained, stockpiled, or sent coal to areas requiring it; Ordnance and Hydrography dealt directly with the mines to supply its ordnance works.

When Orders and Detail took over the management of coal, it consigned supplies to the commanding officers of stations, who delivered it on requisition to forces afloat. After 30 June 1863, Orders and Detail kept a running inventory of quantities on hand in domestic piles and in ships abroad.[2] In July 1863, only 170 tons were received from the mines for ships and stations in South Carolina and Georgia, whereas the Charleston command alone required two hundred tons for an average month.[3] Ships had to burn wood except when going into action. Wood cutting parties were sent ashore and wood was stacked all over the ships.

Ships were handicapped by fuel shortage throughout the war. Efforts to stockpile large quantities ashore or in hulks afloat were futile; there was seldom enough coal to supply current needs, particularly of the desirable, almost smokeless anthracite.

---

2. Circular of Orders and Detail, 1 October 1863, Emory Special Collections.
3. McCorkle to Tattnall, 22 August 1863, Savannah Squadron Papers, #156, Emory Special Collections.

7

The Office of Ordnance and Hydrography: General

Officers in Charge
   Captain Duncan N. Ingraham: 10 June 1861–16 November 1861
   Commander George Minor: December 1861–March 1863
   Commander John M. Brooke: March 1863–end of war

THE function of the Office of Ordnance and Hydrography was to design, develop, purchase, produce, test, distribute, and provide for the maintenance of guns, ammunition, ordnance stores, tools, pyrotechnics, and navigation instruments. It was responsible for chart production and distribution, the collection and dissemination of other hydrographic information, the maintenance of aids to navigation, and the formal training of midshipmen.[1] The unofficial Department directory of 18 July 1861 indicated that the Confederate officer in charge of Ordnance and Hydrography also was responsible for the business of the former Bureau of Construction and Repair (ships) and Bureau of Yards and Docks (shore installations).[2] This assignment appears nowhere else and probably was not fulfilled.

   The first officer in charge was Captain Duncan N. Ingraham, a courtly, slow-thinking, elderly officer from a dis-

---

1. *C. S. Navy Department General Orders*, 8 June 1863; 18 July 1863.
2. Vanfelson, 10.

tinguished Charleston family. He had served in the United States Navy for forty-eight years. An opponent of secession, devoted to the traditions of the United States Navy, and openly critical of Stephen R. Mallory, he was nevertheless an excellent head of the Confederacy's Office of Ordnance and Hydrography. From 1856 to August 1860 he had been Chief of the Bureau of Ordnance and Hydrography, following which he had been assigned command of the USS *Richmond* in the Mediterranean. He served the Confederacy briefly at Pensacola before becoming officer in charge of Ordnance and Hydrography. No doubt Chief Clerk Joseph P. McCorkle, who had been Chief Clerk of the United States Bureau of Ordnance and Hydrography, helped Ingraham in establishing and maintaining an efficient organization. Ingraham surrounded himself with outstanding officers and allowed them wide discretion. The reason for Ingraham's departure from Richmond is unknown, but it is likely that he sought transfer to Charleston in order to have a more active part in the fighting in his home state.

Commander George Minor of Virginia, who had served as Ingraham's office assistant, relieved him in December 1861. An officer of thirty-three years experience in the old navy, Minor was elder brother of Lieutenant Robert D. Minor, also an ordnance specialist. Commander Minor was a capable, efficient officer, who was soon eclipsed by his brilliant assistant, John M. Brooke.

Brooke was one of the few men in the Confederate States Navy who showed genius during the Civil War. A young man when compared with his predecessors, Brooke had entered the United States Navy in 1841 and was one of the earliest graduates of the naval academy. He was the inventor of a deep sea sounding device which he was using for the survey of the North Pacific when the Civil War started. Brooke resigned and at once began the two projects which brought him promotion to commander over the heads of half the lieutenants in the Confederacy: the *Merrimack* and the Brooke gun. Brooke continued in office through the remainder of the war, his inquiring mind studying scientific publications he ordered from abroad, devising practical tests of his ideas, open to suggestion, eager to improve old ways or to admit error when it occurred. Brooke's letters are clear, responsible, and orderly.

He was punctilious about giving credit to others when he could have received it for himself merely by keeping quiet. His subordinates included a number of outstanding men who had once been his seniors, and they worked faithfully and well for him in the Confederacy and with him in later life.

8

The Office of Ordnance and
Hydrography: Ordnance

THE Office of Ordnance and Hydrography maintained control of ordnance equipment on inventory, set production goals, made contracts for foreign and domestic production, kept records on the performances of guns, established allowances of training ammunition, gave technical advice for maintenance and operation of its equipment, and exchanged information with the army. Its organization included an officer in charge, an assistant officer in charge, an inspector of ordnance, a draftsman, and two or more clerks.

The ordnance installations were of varying characteristics and capabilities and often had to undertake activities not rightly their own. Navy yards were expected to perform every naval industrial function except manufacture powder. Naval ordnance works manufactured guns, gun carriages, armor plate, and solid shot. Naval ordnance laboratories assembled fuses, primers, and explosive shells. The navy powder mill manufactured and assembled propulsion charges and pyrotechnics.

It was expected that each industrial installation would maintain its own quality control system, but the Inspector of Ordnance (Commander Archibald B. Fairfax) was entitled to inspect samples from any station. A station was set up on James Island to prove projectiles against armor. Tests were conducted with up to double charge to insure safety of gun and projectile. Each gun was stamped with a serial number and was accompanied by a card on which was entered its full history, including the weight and type of powder of each shot. The Office of Ordnance and Hydrography required a complete account of any malfunction of the gun.

Since a large proportion of the ordnance officers of the United States Navy became Confederate naval ordnance officers, organization, operating methods, and official manual carried over intact. Commissioned ordnance officers in the navy were not a special corps; they served in normal shipboard capacities when not assigned specifically to ordnance duties.

Staffs of flag officers afloat included ordnance officers whose duties were to supervise installation of new guns in ships, to determine the status of guns and ammunition in the squadron, to advise the weight of charge and kind of projectiles to be fired, and to help decide upon the target for each ship. The executive officer of a ship was the vessel's gunnery officer in battle. He picked out the ship's target, determined ammunition to be used against it, and directed battery officers.

The officer in direct charge of ordnance equipment aboard ship was the gunner. A warrant officer ranking after boatswain and before warranted master's mate, he was eligible to succeed to command. The gunner was in charge of the ammunition magazines, pyrotechnics, firearms, broadswords, and other weapons. He was responsible for the maintenance of the battery aboard ship as well as for such tools and supplies peculiar to his department as rammers and worms, gun tackle, wedges, elevating screws, gunsights (when fitted), greases, and oils. He had a supply of grey, red, and white flannel for making respectively full, first reduced, and second reduced charges of powder.[1] His supply of powder and projectiles ideally amounted to one hundred rounds per gun. Projectiles were round solid shot, cylindrical solid wrought iron or steel bolts with conical noses, cylindrical explosive shell, and quilted grapeshot.

Petty officer assistants of the gunner were armorers, armorer's mates, gunner's mates, and quarter gunners. At battle stations the gunner and gunner's mates issued ammunition and arms, repaired damaged ordnance, and flooded magazines in case of fire. Petty officers of other ratings acted as first and second gun captains in charge of loading and aiming their pieces as ordered by the division lieutenant.

During the time between Virginia's secession and the incorporation of the Virginia state navy into that of the Confederacy on 10 June 1861, the commander of the Norfolk Navy Yard, Captain French Forrest, controlled, prepared, and distributed the 533 heavy guns and 150 tons of gunpowder seized in the yard.[2] The yard produced, assembled, and issued gun carriages, projectiles, and tools as best it could, distributing powder on requisition to battery officers ashore. The system worked because the shore batteries were almost all commanded by former officers of the United States Navy and familiar procedure was used. Management of ordnance by the Norfolk Navy Yard was satisfactory during this period because almost all the heavy guns, equipment, ammunition, and ordnance technicians of the South were in that great navy yard.

After Virginia turned over to the Confederacy her

---

1. *O.R.N.*, ser. 2, II, 472, 480.
2. *Ibid.*, 77.

naval property and men, the Office of Ordnance and Hydrography operated as planned. For the first two years, overseas purchases were made by the Secretary. After Brooke took charge, he corresponded directly with European agents and for a while even had his own temporary European representative, Lieutenant William Murdaugh.

One of the officers commanding a shore battery on the James River was Lieutenant Catesby ap R. Jones, formerly an assistant to Commander John A. Dahlgren of the United States Navy in his experiments with scientifically designed guns. Jones and Lieutenant John Brooke of the Office of Ordnance and Hydrography continued some of the experiments, using as targets sections of armor plate backed by heavy oak. They determined that armor placed at an angle of about 38° from the horizontal offered good protection against projectiles travelling along a flat trajectory. At the same time this angle was steep enough to permit guns to be worked through ports cut in the armor and to give adequate protection to engines and crews. This compromise was one of the break-throughs which made the *Merrimack* possible.

Dahlgren constructed heavy, cumbersome guns with maximum strength in the breech where greatest stress occurred. The Confederacy, short of time and metal, had a large number of heavy old smooth bores from the Norfolk Navy Yard. Brooke rifled these guns and reinforced the breeches by shrinking on three to nine wrought iron bands under stress. Large enough to slide on when heated, they were made a little too small to fit over the gun when cool; therefore when the bands cooled, they squeezed in on the chambered portion of the gun. In some cases a second layer of bands was placed over the first. The theory was simple,

---

3. *Ibid.*, ser. i, XX, 857. Brooke's idea was not original; the British Blakeley gun was made in much the same way, and the British Armstrong was tightly wound with wire to the same purpose.

but the process, which was also used in the manufacture of new guns, required skill and precision.[3]

For the first two years of the war Tredegar Iron Works was the only source for reliable new heavy guns, although a number of New Orleans manufacturers attempted to make them. When the first models in New Orleans failed to meet specifications and the Office of Ordnance and Hydrography refused to accept more guns without rigid test, manufacturers declined to take additional contracts.

Dependence for big guns upon a single firm located near the enemy worried Confederate naval officers. Accordingly in October 1862, they began preparations to make guns in Alabama at the Selma Foundry Works, purchased by the government in February 1863. By May 1863 Lieutenant Catesby ap R. Jones was ordered to Selma to take charge of the naval works for the Office of Ordnance and Hydrography. This industrial plant was intended to roll armor plate as well as to make guns and shells, but Jones never had enough artisans to produce to capacity. Working day and night, Selma could produce only one gun a week.[4]

The first big gun was shipped from Selma on 8 January 1864 and the last went out 22 March 1865. A total of fifteen 6.4 inch, thirty-nine 7 inch, and one 11 inch (the last gun) Brooke rifles were made, plus a number of miscellaneous smaller guns for the navy and army.[5]

Gun carriages, sights, and associated equipment were manufactured in the naval ordnance works in Richmond, Charlotte, Charleston, and Atlanta.[6] After the Atlanta works was moved to Augusta in the summer of 1864, the carriage shop was apparently run as a civilian concern by Millikin and Harnell.[7] The gun carriage required well-seasoned hard wood, careful workmanship, and a good deal of time, and at

4. *Ibid.*, XXI, 874; *O.R.A.*, ser. 4, III, 520–523.
5. Walter W. Stephens, "The Brooke Guns from Selma," *Alabama Historical Quarterly*, XX (1958)), 462–475.
6. *O.R.N.*, ser. 2, II, 250–251, 548, 757; A. P. McCorkle to W. W. Hunter, 15 February 1864, Savannah Squadron Papers #331, Special Collections, Emory.
7. Millikin and Harnell to W. W. Hunter, 15 April 1865, Hunter Papers, Tulane University.

the beginning of the war cost about twice as much as a gun.[8] Some guns were fitted with pivoting carriages which allowed them to make large angular movements in the horizontal plane and thus to utilize the gun port on either side. Power for this movement was applied through a gun tackle, a system of pulleys. Systems to absorb the recoil were relatively ineffective, making it necessary to restrict heavy shipboard guns to angles of elevation of less than 8° whereas similar guns ashore were allowed 15° or more. Elevation was achieved by a screw device, supplemented by levers and wedges. The handling mechanisms and the crude sights of the day (usually made for one special gun) made necessary the expedient of pointing the gun as near the target as feasible and firing when the target crossed the sights. A choice of friction and percussion primers for firing the guns was available.[9]

Naval ordnance works had good reputations for flexibility and cooperation. For example, when General Robert E. Lee asked for a railroad-mounted gun during the peninsula campaign of 1862, Brooke designed and the Richmond Naval Ordnance Works manufactured and assembled a rifled and banded 32-lb. gun and delivered it in less than three weeks.[10]

At the beginning of the war, spherical cannon balls were becoming obsolete. During the 1850's, controversy raged in most of the navies of the world over the use of solid shot or explosive shell. The ironclad, which was in large measure a reply to the effectiveness of shell, brought about a third side in the argument. The solid wrought iron or steel bolt, basically cylindrical but usually with some kind of blunt point, came into use to penetrate armor. This bolt required a rifle to give it the velocity necessary to penetrate a metal shield, while the velocity from a smooth bore

---

8. *O.R.N.*, ser. 2, II, 528.
9. *Ibid.*, ser. 1, XXI, 863, 874, 881.
10. *Ibid.*, VII, 802; *O.R.A.*, ser. 1, XI, pt. 3, 575.

was satisfactory for a shell which might break if it struck armor at high speed. Hence there was a school of thought which favored smooth-bore, shell-firing guns and another which wanted rifled guns that cast bolts. There were also some conservatives who wanted to stick to round shot because they liked to fire ricochet shots at the enemy waterline. Most ships carried a mixture of various types of guns and ammunition.

Supplying solid spherical shot was not a problem, probably because it was obsolescent, relatively easy to make, common to both army and navy, and the only kind of projectile which the United States Navy had stockpiled before the Civil War. A workman at the Charlotte Naval Works devised a machine for turning out good spheres quickly.[11]

Shells were a more difficult problem. Their walls had to be thin enough to allow ample space within for the explosive charge, but strong enough to withstand handling and firing. They had to be free of pores or fissures. Naval Ordnance Works at Norfolk, New Orleans, Atlanta, Charleston, Charlotte, and Richmond made shells in considerable quantity. The works at Selma had machinery for manufacturing shells but lacked the necessary laborers.

The Naval Ordnance Works at Charlotte was the only place in the Confederacy which forged wrought iron bolts for the army or the navy.

Obtaining powder for big naval guns was a vexatious problem in the early part of the war, and powder had to be rationed. In addition to the 150 tons captured at Norfolk there were only small amounts scattered here and there in revenue cutters.

A naval powder mill was established in Petersburg, Virginia, but produced little if any powder before being

---

11. Violet G. Alexander, "The Confederate States Navy Yard at Charlotte, North Carolina, 1862–65," Southern Historical Society *Papers*, XL, 1915, 189.

moved to Columbia, South Carolina, on 15 August 1862.[12] Until 1864 powder from the army or from Europe was required to supplement the navy's production, but after that time the Columbia mill, under its civilian superintendent, P. Baudery Garésche, met the navy's demands. Garésche also improved the quality of his powder through experimental firing conducted at Mobile.[13] The Niter and Mining Bureau supplied saltpeter and otherwise cooperated with the powder mill, although the navy continued to look for its own sources of raw materials.[14]

In the naval ordnance laboratories at Richmond, Charlotte, Atlanta, and New Orleans, wives and daughters of sailors, given preference for this work when practicable, strapped, fuzed, fitted, and prepared shells for use, and packed them for distribution in wooden boxes.[15] They drove fuses and made friction primers and sometimes made up the propulsion charges for the larger guns.[16]

Some of the difficulties experienced in the utilization of ordnance aboard ships were due to a lack of cooperation between the Chief Constructor and the Office of Ordnance and Hydrography in the design of ships. The constructor determined the hull shape; ordnance decided upon the allocation of guns, but neither adequately faced the problem of the best way for the guns to be arranged on the ship. Thick inclined armor backed by heavy beams forced the guns to be made long-barrelled so that the muzzle blast would take place outside the ship. Since the guns were all muzzle loaders (experience in Europe with breech loaders caused the rejection of this type), they had to be run inside the ship to be sponged and loaded. This took an enormous amount of precious deck space and it also called for exact design of gun-handling mechanism. Designs were either lacking, poorly made, or made by one group without ad-

---

12. *O.R.N.*, ser. 2, II, 250.
13. *Ibid.*, 757; ser. 1, XXI, 876.
14. *Ibid.*, ser. 2, II, 550.
15. *Ibid.*, I, 777.
16. *Ibid.*, II, 250–251.

equate consultation with the other.[17] Gun ports were customarily cut after the wooden structure was built, to suit the guns assigned. Whether the responsibility lay with one office or the other, it was clearly the duty of both to seek a sensible solution.

In the realm of surface ordnance, the Office of Ordnance and Hydrography admirably fulfilled its mission. Inheriting obsolescent guns, it made them into efficient weapons; then used the lessons learned to develop new guns. It developed systems of manufacture compatible with the materials and workers available. For lack of labor, it did not produce enough projectiles, especially wrought iron bolts. It conducted an alert research program which included collection of data from England and France. The safety program, testing system, and exchange of information between ordnance officers were all adequate and effective. Except in the matter of artisans, relations with the army, and especially with the Ordnance Bureau and the Niter and Mining Bureau, were cordial and mutually rewarding. The single serious failure—the matter of the mounting of guns—was shared with the Naval Constructor. The navy and the nation were well served by the conventional arms section of the Office of Ordnance and Hydrography.

17. *Ibid.*, ser. 1, XXI, 875; D. P. McCorkle to W. W. Hunter, 15 February 1864, Savannah Squadron Papers #331, Emory Special Collections.

9

The Office of Ordnance and Hydrography: Mine Warfare

THE navy's mines were devised, manufactured, and plant- ed by a small and highly secret organization nominally a part of the Office of Ordnance and Hydrography but relatively independent of that agency.[1] Commander Mat- thew Maury was in charge until 20 June 1862 when Lieu- tenant Hunter Davidson relieved him and Maury went abroad to buy material for mine warfare. Duties and re- sponsibilities of the mine warfare chief overlapped those of Colonel Gabriel J. Rains of the Army Torpedo Bureau. Available records do not indicate the extent to which the two services cooperated during the war, but their relation- ships must have been close. For instance, in 1864 navy launches laid mines in the Savannah area at the request of the local army commander.[2] At other times, naval vessels carried army torpedoes at the ends of spars which they at- tempted to ram into the sides of enemy ships.

In 1874 Davidson claimed that he, not Maury, had in- vented the Confederate mine system.[3] Seven years later he said that he and Maury had done it together and that Colonel Rains had nothing to do with them.[4] Regardless of the originator, the idea was a good one.

---

1. The words torpedo and submarine battery were the terms applied to this weapon during the Civil War.
2. *O.R.N.*, ser. 1, XV, 751, 579, 764.
3. Dunbar Rowland, ed., *Jefferson Davis Constitutionalist: His Letters, Papers, and Speeches* (Jackson, Miss., 1923) VII, 387.
4. *Ibid.*, IX, 19.

The weapons typically consisted of old boilers filled with seventy to three hundred pounds of powder and attached to empty barrels which were anchored to float three to eight feet below the surface of the water. Their ignition charges were connected with galvanic batteries ashore by salvaged telegraph wire, which was insulated with gutta percha. An operator ashore closed the circuit to detonate the charge. Constant vigilance was needed to prevent the enemy from sweeping mines, and for this purpose the boat *Teaser*, with an observation balloon, was provided.[5] The submarine defense force was an independent naval command on the James, directly under the squadron commander.

Thirty-nine Union vessels are said to have been damaged or destroyed by mines.[6] Since there is no way to tell which mines destroyed which ships, and since participants disagreed as to who contributed ideas and devices, it is difficult to assess the navy's role. The navy erred in not pressing to get the mission of obstructing and mining rivers and harbors.

One of the Confederate Navy's misfortunes was the mutual antipathy of Secretary Mallory and Commander Maury. Maury had an almost obsessive interest in mine warfare. He had the scientific background, channels of communication to Europe, and the dogged temperament which should have brought success to his endeavor, but he was openly contemptuous of Mallory.

The feud dated back to 1855 when Mallory's retiring board retired Maury, world famous scientist, because he was not considered qualified for sea duty in his rank. Maury had a crippled leg, and at his own request his time at sea since his entry in the United States Navy in 1825 had been limited to nine years. After retirement he secured his re-

---

5. *O.R.N.*, ser. 1, VII, 543–546.
6. J. Thomas Scharf, *History of the Confederate States Navy* (Albany, 1894) 768.

instatement, but he blamed Mallory for his humiliation.

Maury was an extreme secessionist. In April 1861 he resigned his commission, left the Naval Observatory he had founded and commanded for twenty years, and became a member of the Council of Three to prepare Virginia for war. He thought himself a naval strategist when in fact he was a superb scientist with little more than an amateur's concept of how to fight the war.

Maury worked hard for the creation of a fleet of tiny wooden steamboats, each mounting a single heavy gun. On 23 December 1861 he got an appropriation of $2,000,000 for the project despite the opposition of Mallory, who detested the scheme.[7] The battle between the *Merrimack* and the *Monitor* showed that the little gunboats would not be able to float long enough to do damage. Construction was stopped and the money was diverted to ironclads, but valuable time and money had been wasted.[8]

Maury experimented with mines for some time before he went into operation on the James. In August 1861 he had plans to mine the Mississippi River if he could find a deep place with stagnant water at the bottom which would not wash out his minefield.[9] Maury would not plead for his program to Mallory, and Mallory was not interested enough to start it by himself.

Had the Confederate Navy grasped the possibilities of mine warfare in 1861, it should have been able to hold the estuaries of the Chesapeake Bay and possibly the navigable sounds of North Carolina. These were of mineable depth and had but slight currents. The Confederacy would not have been able to manufacture enough mines to sink every ship that tried to enter, but it could have threatened all and sunk a few, and so have impeded navigation.

Maury established his organization, instructed Lieu-

---

7. *O.R.N.*, ser. 2, II, 117.
8. *Ibid.*, I, 751.
9. *Ibid.*, ser. 1, XXII, 791.

tenant Hunter Davidson and Lieutenant Robert D. Minor in the construction and maintenance of mines, and then on about 1 October 1862 sailed for Europe. He continued his experiments, and sent back materials and devices, but he lost his intense interest in mines and became more a philosopher and propagandist than a designer and maker of munitions.

10

The Office of Ordnance and Hydrography: Hydrography

THE Office of Ordnance and Hydrography was responsible for the collection, presentation, and distribution of navigational information and equipment. It also had responsibility for aids to navigation.

No information could be found as to the specific assignments to hydrographic duty within the Office of Ordnance and Hydrography. Two officers of the rank of master were in the office in 1862 and three in 1864, any of whom might have been given the responsibility. Mallory signed the few letters on the subject which came from the department.

Confederate maritime policy was defensive, and aids to navigation were considered likely to be of more help to an invading enemy than of use to Confederate forces. Therefore, lighthouses were darkened, buoys taken from station, and lightships brought into port for conversion to other uses. Generally speaking, captains were left to their own devices and to the skill or luck of pilots; the Office of Ordnance and Hydrography offered little help.

A commanding officer was more intimately involved in navigation than in any other department of his ship. At sea he often took his own star sights. His assistant for navigation was the master. The duty assignment of master was usually filled by a passed midshipman awaiting promotion to lieutenant or by an officer of the rank of master who might or might not be eligible for promotion.

The master was responsible for maintenance of the charts and navigational instruments as well as for some other stores and items of seamanship. Essentially he was an aide to his commanding officer. Assistants to the master were master's mates, quartermaster, and yeoman.

Another member of the navigation department, most vital in inshore waters although not a regular uniformed member of the ship's company, was the pilot. Probably no other problem in the Confederate Navy was as vexatious as that of the pilots.

By 1860 United States warships were directed to take pilots only when requisite for the safety of the ship, and to release them as soon as practicable, paying the usual commercial rates. This system was carried over into the Confederate States Navy.[1] The rates were usually dependent upon tonnage and distance travelled. On the longer rivers, like the Mississippi, commercial steamboats usually hired their pilots by the month, as long as the vessel remained in waters with which the pilot was familiar. The practice of hiring river pilots on a monthly basis eventually was made legal for the Confederate Navy. Lieutenant W. H. Parker stated that he proposed incorporating pilots in the navy as officers, but that his recommendation was rejected.[2]

A pilot is essentially a mariner with specialized knowledge of a particular stretch of water. This may be a harbor or an inland passage between islands; it may extend over a distance of many miles along a river or for a short distance over a shoal spot. A vessel contemplating a long voyage

---

1. *Digest*, 219.
2. William H. Parker, *Recollections of a Naval Officer, 1841–1865* (New York, 1883), 284. Hereafter cited as Parker, *Recollections*. He was not entirely correct; a few were appointed masters or master's mates.

in shallow or restricted areas frequently had several pilots for each stretch of water so that she could proceed without interruption.

A frequently overlooked feature of the Civil War is the ignorance of American naval and military officers of the geography of their own country. A vast coastal survey of the United States had been underway since 1853, but few of the charts had been published. Matthew Fontaine Maury, the world's greatest oceanographer and in charge of the United States Navy's Hydrographic Office for fifteen years before the Civil War, boasted of bringing no charts with him to the Confederacy when he resigned.[3] He brought practically no shallow water knowledge, either. Commanders Sidney Smith Lee and William T. Muse, who came South from duty in the Washington office of the Coast Survey, did no better. Fortunately a number of the naval officers who had been shunted aside from the navy to duties in Light House Service or to ships of the Coast Survey or who had been members of the Revenue Service also entered the Confederate Navy. These officers, who could practically act as their own pilots, included most of the best cruiser captains and blockade runners.

Probably nothing will make a daring captain more cautious than the fear of grounding in unfamiliar waters; few military occurrences are of more immediately disastrous consequences than stranding in the presence of an enemy. Without adequate charts and usually without specialized knowledge of local waters, the captains were dependent upon their pilots. Sometimes, as in the case of the Yazoo and Mississippi pilots aboard the *Arkansas*, the captain was justified in proceeding with boldness and confidence. Captain Isaac Brown gave great praise to pilots J. R. Shacklett, J. G. Hodges, J. L. Brady, and a Mr. Gil-

---

3. Diana Fontaine Maury Corbin, *A Life of Matthew Fontaine Maury* (London, 1888), 196.

mer, who on 15 July 1862 helped him run his ironclad into Vicksburg through two Union fleets.[4] Other times, battles depended upon the weak support of the halfhearted or excitable, the foreign or Yankee-born, or, not infrequently, a Negro slave experienced in running a rice flat among the Sea Islands.[5] That some of these men loyally and efficiently performed their duties (Moses Dallas, colored pilot of the *Savannah*, died a hero) could not have reassured the captains; in close quarters a single turn of the wheel could run a ship hard aground or keep her off. Buchanan, Catesby ap R. Jones, and Tattnall, successively captains of the *Merrimack*, all blamed faint-hearted pilots for the failure of that ironclad to do more damage.[6] Raphael Semmes had to force pilots aboard the *Sumter* in 1861 as he prepared to run the Mississippi River blockade to sea.[7] Desertion of pilots was common, and the loss to the Confederate Navy was compounded by the fact that the specialized skills of the absconding pilots usually were placed at the disposal of the enemy.

Southern naval officers may be excused for failure to know their own waters in early 1861, but it is incredible that those few possessing local knowledge were not better used. None of the senior Confederate naval officers at the Battle of New Orleans had ever previously done duty on the Mississippi, while both David G. Farragut and David D. Porter of the Union navy were well acquainted with the river. Likewise, after four years of war, commanding officers of ships of the James River Squadron were still dependent upon pilots, some the same men suspected of cowardice on the *Merrimack* in 1862.[8]

Why did Confederate naval officers not learn the rivers? Officers were moved so often that, by the time a commanding officer became familiar with his ship and her environ-

---

4. *O.R.N.*, ser. 1, XIX, 69.
5. *Ibid.*, XVI, 498; Savannah Squadron Papers #159.
6. *O.R.N.*, ser. 1, VI, 991; VII, 754, 793; X, 629.
7. Semmes, 109.
8. *O.R.N.*, ser. 1, VII, 336–337; XI, 678.

ment, he was transferred to a ship or station in another location. The failure of the Confederate Navy to provide itself with adequate and trustworthy navigators during four years of war was catastrophic.

On 11 March 1864, the Confederate Navy took its only really effective step in the hydrographic field when Mallory ordered Lieutenant John Wilkinson to duty in Wilmington, North Carolina. Wilkinson, a naval officer since 1837, was one of the most successful blockade runners in the Confederacy. He was daring, resourceful, and knowledgeable. Given broad command and liaison powers at Wilmington as well as detailed instructions concerning hydrography, Wilkinson had seventy men with whom to establish and maintain a system of lights, buoys, and other aids to navigation up and down the coast from the entrance to Wilmington. He was to collect information on depth of water in the various channels, check it from time to time, and give incoming and outgoing vessels the latest data. He was directed to examine the qualifications of pilots and give them certificates stating their abilities.[9] Wilkinson was also given vague authority over blockade running vessels.

This organization performed well for a few months; then Wilkinson was transferred from one to another command afloat and ashore for the rest of the war while his hydrographic office at Wilmington was in the hands of various inexperienced assistants. He deplored these erratic changes of duty, but he served efficiently wherever he was ordered.[10] His skill, originality, and leadership would have been invaluable had he been permitted to supervise blockade running in accordance with his orders and desires.

---

9. *Ibid.*, IX, 804.
10. John Wilkinson, *The Narrative of a Blockade Runner* (New York, 1877), 169, 210.

11

The Office of Ordnance and Hydrography: The Naval School

Superintendent: Lieutenant William H. Parker, May 1863–
end of war
Commandant of Midshipmen
Lieutenant Benjamin P. Loyall: May 1863–Fall 1863
Lieutenant James H. Rochelle: Fall 1863–end of war

T H E mission of the naval school was to prepare assigned
midshipmen in the professional and cultural subjects
covered in examinations for promotion to lieutenant. As
successor to the United States Naval Academy, it received
midshipmen in all stages of naval education, and the intent
was to approach as near as practicable to the familiar system
of instruction at Annapolis. There were two theoretically
independent phases in the life of a midshipman: the completion of the required course of education, and the successful passing of annual examinations conducted by a
board of senior officers not connected with the school.

An act of the Confederate Congress of 16 March 1861
authorized the President to appoint as many midshipmen
as he deemed necessary. An amendment a month later set
the maximum number at 106.[1] The military rank of mid-

---

1. *C. S. Navy Register 1863*, 30, 38.

shipmen continued whether they were on duty with the rest of the navy or were in an educational institution.

Mallory intended to start a naval school in 1862 aboard the old frigate *United States*, but her loss when the Norfolk Navy Yard was abandoned required postponement of the project until a suitable location could be found. He directed Lieutenant William H. Parker to recommend a site in North Carolina, but then decided to use the partially armored steamer *Patrick Henry* in the James River. In May 1863 he assigned Parker superintendent of the naval school. Parker had been in the second class to enter the United States Naval Academy for the complete course, and had served there as an instructor in seamanship for about a year following his graduation in 1847. He was the author of a textbook on naval light artillery; another of his textbooks, *Elements of Seamanship*, was in use by both sides during the Civil War.

The desire of the Navy Department was to send the midshipmen to a suitable location and teach them seamanship, astronomy, navigation, English, mathematics, physics, history, a foreign language, drawing and drafting, infantry tactics, and a catch-all called ethics. Half the instructors would be naval officers and half would be civilian experts in their fields. When a midshipman was graduated and considered ready for promotion, he would be ordered before a board of senior officers for examination of his academic and professional progress, his proficiency on any sea duty that he had performed, and his moral and mental aptitude for an officer's career in the Confederate Navy.

Early in 1861, President Davis made an initial appointment of approximately fifty midshipmen. Later, additional appointments were made to raise the total throughout the war to about two hundred. According to regulations, these young men had to be between fourteen and eighteen years old at the time of appointment, had to be able to pass a fairly stringent physical examination, and had to present evidence of good character. Many of the appointees were sons of naval officers; one of them was Mallory's son. In January 1865, the total number of midshipmen allowed was raised to 150 in order to fill fleet needs after allowing for the expected fifty per cent attrition over the four-year course.

The approximately fifty midshipmen retained aboard CSS *Patrick Henry* participated in normal classroom recitations. Their instructors included:

Lieutenant Wilburn B. Hall, professor of astronomy and navigation

Lieutenant Thomas W. W. Davis, assistant professor of navigation

Lieutenant Oscar F. Johnston, professor of astronomy, navigation, and surveying

Lieutenant Charles J. Graves, instructor of seamanship

Lieutenant J. W. Billups, assistant instructor of seamanship

Lieutenant William V. Comstock, instructor of gunnery

Master George M. Peek, professor of mathematics

John P. McGuire, assistant professor of mathematics

Master G. W. Armistead, professor of physics

Master Lewis Huck, professor of English

Master George A. Peple, professor of German, French, and history (a German citizen)

Master Sauxey, professor of infantry tactics and sword exercises

Assistant Surgeons W. J. Addison and James G. Bixley

Paymaster William M. Ladd

Second Assistant Engineer E. G. Hall

Boatswain Andrew Blakie

Gunners E. R. Johnson and William F. Brittingham
Sailmaker William Bennett[2]

Instruction, held on deck or in two small compartments between the paddle wheels, was often punctuated by gunfire from nearby friendly shore batteries or ships' guns. Occasionally Federal ships or field pieces would bring the *Patrick Henry* under fire. Frequently some of or all the midshipmen were moved ashore to augment or relieve naval batteries on Drewry's Bluff, but there was no reduction in academic standards. The marking system of the United States Naval Academy (4.0 excellent, 2.5 passing) was used.

Midshipmen wore officers' uniforms with three medium-size buttons on the cuff and a fouled anchor on the cap. Their food was the plain, monotonous food of the James River Squadron with an occasional ration of coffee or tea.

It was planned that, following the December 1864 graduation, the new midshipmen fourth class (freshmen) and new first class (seniors) would remain on the schoolship, about sixty all told, while the remaining twenty-four served aboard warships or resided in extra cabins to be built on Drewry's Bluff. To what extent these plans were put into effect is not known. Lieutenant Parker's command of sixty midshipmen, ten officers, and thirty colored servants went South with the President on 2 April 1865. Mallory clung to the idea of continuing the school in North Carolina or Georgia, and to this end he directed Parker to find a suitable place for it.[3]

Midshipmen aboard warships were expected to keep up their studies in addition to performing their ordinary watch and division duties as junior officers. A general order from the Navy Department required that they be aboard each liberty day by sunset and that they maintain their

---

2. William H. Parker, "The Confederate Navy," in Clement A. Evans, ed., *Confederate Military History* (Atlanta, 1899) XII, 96; *C. S. Navy Register 1864*.

3. Parker, *Recollections*, 347.

journals and other notebook work. The journals contained astronomical and meteorological data, narratives of happenings, discussions of problems, solutions of seamanship evolutions, and descriptions of rigging or gunnery practices. Frequently exercises consisted of a list of questions and answers, beginning with a hair-raising predicament at sea from which the midshipman was supposed to save his ship.[4]

In April 1862, a board of senior officers not attached to the naval school met to examine all acting midshipmen and assign them classes. Other similarly constituted examining boards which convened in March 1863, December 1863, and December 1864 were directed to meet in the principal naval ports and in Europe to examine all midshipmen whether attached to the school or not.

Different classes were to be examined as follows:
First class (senior) upon navigation, seamanship, naval and infantry tactics, naval gunnery, steam machinery, modern languages, drawing and drafting.
Second class (juniors) upon the same branches but not so critically.
Third class (sophomores) upon practical seamanship, naval tactics, naval gunnery, mathematics, ancient and modern history, ethics and English studies, French, drawing and drafting.
Fourth class (freshmen) upon mathematics, exercise of great guns and small arms, ethics, and English studies and drawing.

New acting midshipmen appointed subject to examination were to receive physical examinations, exhibit evidences of good moral character, be able to read and write well, spell with correctness, add, subtract, multiply, and divide.[5]

The naval school did its work well. Twenty-nine for-

4. *O.R.N.*, ser. 1, XV, 709.
5. *C. S. Navy Register 1864*, 82–83; Examination papers, Emory Special Collections (n.p., but apparently Richmond, 1864).

mer United States Navy midshipmen and thirty others had passed their promotion examinations by November 1864. About forty were scheduled to graduate the following December, making a total of almost a hundred graduates. They were well behaved, reliable young men. The march to the South, after Richmond was abandoned in 1865, was a test of the character of the young men, and they stood it well. Every report of that journey paid tribute to the staunch behavior of these young officers. The school, the South, and the navy had cause to be proud of the midshipmen.

The question remains: Was it sensible to conduct such a naval school in view of the South's plight in 1861–1865?

In view of the severe shortage in manpower, the Confederacy could hardly spare the excellent lieutenants who operated the school and the midshipmen who attended it. True, the midshipmen might enter at an age far below the conscript limit, but they stayed in the school four years. It should have been clear that a naval school in which an able-bodied male was expected to spend four years would not produce many officers during the short war most people expected or even the long war that actually occurred. The midshipmen were training for a post-war navy. The Confederacy was from its beginning in too precarious a position to concern itself unduly with the distant future. It had a war to win first.

The school course was too long and too good for what the navy could expect to get out of it during the Civil War. By the time the school was underway in 1863, even such things as celestial navigation were extraneous to the junior officer's career. The Civil War was a river and harbor war, but naval officers persisted in thinking in terms of sails and sextants, foreign languages, history and ethics, items of use over a long career at sea, but of little value to a junior officer in a beleaguered, landlocked navy.

A more realistic naval administration would have discarded the traditions and natural desires of professional naval officers who wanted to continue the standards of excellence they had achieved. The Confederate Navy should have been satisfied with practically trained young officers whom it could produce in short time. The curriculum should have been made spare but intensive, with only a few midshipmen at a time and two or three officers to instruct them for two or three months.

As it was, the school occupied a ship and her crew in the crowded James River, and cost money and used supplies that might have been applied to ends more directly related to winning the war.

12

The Office of Provisions and Clothing: General

Officer in Charge
Paymaster John De Bree: 1861–April 1864
Paymaster James A. Semple: April 1864–April 1865
T. C. De Leon, Chief Clerk: entire war

THE Office of Provisions and Clothing was responsible for procuring, distributing, and accounting for the food and uniforms of the navy. It provided the sundry items required for everyday living aboard ship. Its members acted as pay officers, and, generally, as the fiscal agents of the navy.[1]

Paymaster John De Bree, who had served in the United States Navy for forty-four years, was an accommodating man, but he was old, conservative, and increasingly dependent upon Paymaster James A. Semple, whom he brought to Richmond from the *Merrimack* after that vessel was destroyed. Semple, a son-in-law of ex-President Tyler, had been in the United States Navy for seventeen years. He was aggressive, universally admired, a thoroughly competent man for his job. He was one of the last men known to have control over the Confederate treasure before it disappeared in April 1865.

---

1. The senior officer of this corps aboard ship or station, even if by rank an assistant paymaster, was called the paymaster, and the term will be thus used in this chapter.

Two ranks of officers were commissioned in the pay branch: paymaster and assistant paymaster. The eleven paymasters originally appointed were all United States Navy pursers. They were assigned to the more important shore stations and to major staffs. None of the assistant paymasters had naval service prior to entry in the Confederate Navy.

In order to be commissioned an assistant paymaster, an applicant had to be twenty-one to thirty years old, to pass an examination before a board of three paymasters, to prove that he could keep a ship's books, and to present letters testifying to his good character. Promotion from assistant paymaster to paymaster was by seniority. Both paymasters and assistant paymasters had to be bonded. A paymaster with more than twelve years ranked with commander, one with less than that ranked with lieutenant. An assistant paymaster with more than five years ranked after a lieutenant, and one with less than five years was next after a master.[2]

A third grade of pay officer was clerk to a paymaster, an appointed (not commissioned) officer, who ranked with midshipman.[3] The paymaster's clerk was appointed by the captain on the recommendation of the paymaster, and the appointment could be terminated by the captain if the paymaster requested it.[4] A clerk had to be at least eighteen years old.

The paymaster was responsible for requisitioning, storing, issuing, maintaining, and accounting for food, clothing, "small stores" (jackknives, needles, tobacco, mustard, and other items sailors might need for personal use). With the approval of the commanding officer, he requisitioned, received, safeguarded, and paid out money to individuals in the crew. He paid contractors when there was no naval agent or naval storekeeper.

---

2. *C. S. Navy Regulations*, 8.
3. *Ibid.*, 6.
4. *Ibid.*, 9.

Petty officers in the pay branch were the ship's steward and ship's cook. The steward was responsible for provisions in store and for issuing them to the cook or to the mess cooks (men appointed by their mess to draw the mess rations and to prepare and serve the food not cooked by the cook). The cook prepared bread, meat, soup, puddings, and other mass-produced items.

Naval agents were civilian representatives of the Office of Provisions and Clothing whose duty it was to acquire items for use throughout the navy. These men were empowered to make contracts with manufacturers, to purchase directly from producers, and, late in the war, to establish factories and to barter or impress materials urgently required. They also provided transportation for individuals traveling under orders and paid claims resulting from travel.

Material acquired by the naval agents was sent to naval storehouses or directly to the commands by which it was to be used. There were three naval storehouses under the charge of naval storekeepers, civilians who were bonded and paid not more than $1700 a year. The most important storehouse was at Charlotte, North Carolina, and the others were at Albany, Georgia, and Mobile, Alabama. In addition, supply departments for local use were maintained in the various naval stations, yards, and industrial establishments. Storekeepers or officers in charge sent periodic reports to the Office of Provisions and Clothing, which ordered redistribution of stores from time to time.

The Office of Provisions and Clothing was not the only part of the navy which acquired, stored, or delivered materials. Coal, rope, sails, and wood were bought by the Office of Orders and Detail. Ordnance material and navigational instruments were responsibilities of the Office of Ordnance and Hydrography. The Marine Corps handled its own material, as did the Office of Medicine and Surgery. The details of these items are discussed under the appropriate office.

Once items reached a ship, the officer of the deck was responsible for getting them on board and for logging the quantity received. The master was required to supervise storing of all items except ammunition, utilizing a stowage plan worked out in cooperation with the navy yard and kept posted in the front of the log. He had to shift provisions and other stores as necessary to see that the oldest items were used first. Casks and other dunnage were saved and sold and the proceeds put in a "slush fund" to be used for buying special clothing for cooks, side boys, and messengers.[5]

Stores belonging to the boatswain's department (rope, anchors, boat tillers), the carpenter's (lumber), the sailmaker's (sail cloth), and that part of the gunner's which was not arms or ammunition (grease, leather), were turned over to the custody of the yeoman.

The spirits and navigational material were kept by the master. Coal was in custody of either the executive officer or the paymaster and was issued in small lots to the engineer officer. The marine officer retained marine stores, including uniforms, in his own small storeroom. The paymaster's money was kept in an iron strongbox and he was furnished suitable containers for his books and accounts. Commanding officers were ordered to keep a month's supply of stores aboard their ships, but maintenance of this level became increasingly difficult during the latter part of the war.

The commandant responsible for commissioning a ship was required to furnish the commanding officer with an inventory of the stores on board; and, from that time on, the commanding officer (with his clerk doing the work) main-

---

5. *Ibid.*, 81.

tained an expense book which he was required to turn over to his relief when detached. Once every three months he also had to submit to his immediate superior a report of expenses for the preceding quarter.[6]

---

6. *Ibid.*, 64, 79–80.

13

The Office of Provisions and Clothing: Provisions and Stores

THE Confederate Navy adopted the United States Navy ration system but was compelled slowly to modify it. A law of 1842 specified the quantity and type, but not the quality, of food to be issued. Great emphasis was placed on salt pork or beef, rice, and dried peas or beans—items which would keep a long time at sea. Fresh fruit and vegetables were to be furnished in port, with the medical officers always encouraging their use.

The men were to form themselves into messes of eight to fourteen and were not supposed to change mess oftener than once a month. A mess cook was appointed by the members of each mess, and it was he who drew the rations for his fellows. A part of the mess ration could be commuted to money for the purchase of mustard, pepper, and other spices and small stores from the paymaster or from merchants ashore. Hospitals were given special food allowances, free of the usual regulations.[1]

The cook got his supplies from the steward according to a menu approved by the commanding officer. Each man was allowed a gill of spirits or a half pint of wine per day, or he could commute his spirits ration into cash at a rate

---

1. *C. S. Navy Regulations,* 133–138.

of four cents per day—later raised to ten cents, and finally to twenty-two cents. The captain could order or the medical officer could recommend that a man's spirit ration be commuted if either thought this measure necessary.[2]

Scarcity of food was almost always a serious problem within the Confederacy, except for the men on cruisers, who sometimes had excellent food from their prizes. Laws allowing government impressment were extended to the navy, and representatives were sent on the unpleasant mission of seizing provisions from farmers and other producers. The navy ate better than the army for several reasons. The ships (except for the James River Squadron) were far from the immense concentrations of men in the Army of Northern Virginia and the Army of Tennessee, which would have taxed even a better system than the poor one that the army commissary possessed. The cruisers sometimes brought in coffee, tea, and sugar—which were turned in to the naval hospitals, the general navy store, or bartered for other provisions. Cloth was also sometimes used for trading purposes. The navy seems to have had an alert and efficient organization that was flexible enough to meet changing conditions.

Many items on the ration list, such as cheese, butter, and raisins, were never obtainable, and tea and coffee were procurable only through cruisers or at exhorbitant rates from blockade runners.

The navy was eating so well in April 1864 that Paymaster De Bree was constrained, in the interest of interservice harmony, to recommend appointment of a board to review the navy ration and reduce it.[3] In the summer of 1864, the army commissary department was given responsibility for furnishing all provisions to the navy.[4]

In the fall of 1863, the Office of Provisions and Clothing directed Navy Agent William F. Howell in Augusta, Geor-

---

2. *Ibid.*, 136.
3. *O.R.N.*, ser. 2, II, 644.
4. *Ibid.*, 762.

gia, to collect as much wheat as possible and have it ground at Augusta and Montgomery. Howell acquired and ground 1,100 to 1,200 barrels, had some of it baked into ship's bread, and reported his office ready to deliver ten barrels of bread a day at a total cost of fifteen cents a loaf.[5] Even in October 1864, the navy had six to eight months supply of bread on hand and had lent the army 620 barrels of flour.[6] By December 1864, a navy-run flour, grist, and bread establishment was in operation at Albany, Georgia, under the charge of Nelson Tift, Mallory's old friend, now an assistant paymaster in the navy.[7] A week before Appomattox the naval storehouse at Charlotte held such large quantities of flour that Lieutenant W. H. Parker, on his way south with the Confederate treasure, was able to issue his seventy midshipmen and sailors several months' supply.[8]

Fresh meat was not always obtainable on the ships, though even the James River Squadron received meat three days a week in 1864. Salt beef, salt pork, or bacon was almost always served at least four days a week, about one and a quarter pounds a day per man. Some salt meat was brought in from Europe, but the naval agents bought or cured much of the navy's needs. Howell even bought two hundred live hogs, contracted for four hundred more, and bought several hundred sacks of salt in the fall of 1863 in order to be ready for hog-killing time that year.[9] About the same time Paymaster W. W. J. Kelly of the Savannah station set up a similar meat-packing establishment at Albany, Georgia.[10]

The spirit ration was highly controversial. Navy regulations, long custom, and the surgeons of the navy all upheld the issuance of a spirit ration. The doctors thought it should be served with breakfast. Buchanan had quinine put into the rations at Mobile to prevent fever. Because Buchanan opposed liquor aboard ship, he may have used the

5. *Ibid.*, 643.
6. *Ibid.*, 762.
7. Message of the President, January 4, 1865 (Broadside), Emory Special Collections.
8. Parker, *Recollections*, 355.
9. *O.R.N.*, ser. 2, II, 557.
10. *Ibid.*, 553.

bitter-tasting drug partly as a temperance measure. Paymaster De Bree opposed the issuance on both moral and practical grounds. Liquor for either medicine or rations was hard to get. Confederate state governments generally opposed diversion of grain to distilleries. The central government contended that state laws should not interfere with the war effort, and countered objections to diversion of food by proposing to distill only spoiled grain. A distillery at Augusta, Georgia, was built and operated by Naval Agent Howell. Other distilleries were planned at Wilson, North Carolina, Albany, Georgia, and at an unstated location in South Carolina.[11]

Spirits aboard ship were stored separately from the remainder of the provisions and were kept in the custody of the master. The spirit room was opened only in the presence of a commissioned officer and by the authority of the commanding officer. Special care had to be taken against both fire and thirst. Sailors used every possible pretext to get extra liquor, and many if not most of the disciplinary troubles of the navy were associated with alcohol.

For officers, both food and spirit rations were commuted into credit or cash at the rate of twenty-five cents per day, and the officer paid his share of the cost of the mess to which he belonged.[12] Commanding or flag officers had their own messes; the lieutenants and officers of equivalent rank ate in the wardroom, and the rest of the officers belonged to the steerage mess. On small ships, messes were combined. Navy regulations forbade the officers messes' buying provisions from the crew's mess, except on foreign stations.

The separate officers' mess system seems to have persisted on most ships throughout the war, although it is logical to believe that officers' messes must have bought ship's supply whether the vessel was abroad or not. Officers at-

---

11. Frederick S. Daniel, ed., *The Richmond Examiner During the War* (Richmond, 1868), 168; *O.R.A.*, ser. 4, III, 879; *O.R.N.*, ser. 2, II, 553–554, 759.

12. *U. S. Navy Register 1860*, 160.

tached to the ironclads seem to have eaten their meals ashore except when action was imminent. Beginning 17 February 1864, officers were permitted to draw their rations in kind, while attached to a ship.[13] When inflation brought hardship to the families of officers, efforts to extend the army's ration regulations to the navy were successful; and, on 26 November 1864, commissioned, warrant, and appointed officers on shore duty were allowed the same rations, quarters, and fuel allowances as their counterparts in the army. Rations were no longer commuted into cash, nor could one person buy the ration of another.[14] Rations received in the hospital were not charged to the officer.

Considering the severe shortages in much of the Confederacy for most of the war, the navy was notably successful in furnishing provisions and stores. No doubt its mobility, small size, and dispersed nature as well as its captures helped ease the food problem for the navy, but much credit must be given the initiative and ingenuity of navy agents and paymasters.

---

13. *Digest*, 94.
14. *O.R.N.*, ser. 2, II, 775–776.

14

The Office of Provisions and Clothing: Uniforms

ACCORDING to regulations in effect at the beginning of the war, officers were required to furnish their own uniforms. Neither money allowance nor central procurement was contemplated. Uniform regulations are reproduced in the Appendix.

Sailors were to be issued clothing upon entry into the service, and replacements for garments worn out or lost were to be provided aboard ship from stock furnished by naval agents. A man was given a clothing allowance against which issues were charged.[1] At the end of his enlistment, a man was supposed to be paid the amounts not expended.[2] Inspections were held to see that each man had a full bag of properly marked clothing. The men's gear was laid out on deck and the division lieutenant was supposed to count each item for each man and submit a list of deficiencies to the commanding officer, with recommendations as to items which should be issued. The commanding officer approved or disapproved the items, signed the list, and sent it to the paymaster, who issued the approved items, checking each man's pay. When a man in debt badly needed clothing for his health and comfort, the commanding officer could order

---

1. For the initial allowance, see Appendix.
2. *Digest*, 201.

an issue made; otherwise, the man had to get along without it or make his own uniform from scraps of old sail or other scavenged material. The custom of tailoring for oneself was an old one among sailors; it soon became a necessity in the Confederacy.

The system required modifications as the blockade drew tighter. Officers wore their blue United States Navy uniforms. Officers in Europe were the best dressed in the Confederate Navy. They sometimes looked so dapper upon their return to the Confederacy that they gave away some of their garments or changed back to faded old uniforms. Tailors, wives, or mothers made uniforms, at first from cloth approximately the regulation type; eventually they altered old suits, overcoats, or other garments. After 16 January 1865, owing to the scarcity of domestic cloth and the prohibitive costliness of that run through the blockade, officers on active service were permitted to buy cloth or uniforms from the paymaster at cost. One uniform a year was allowed officers below the rank of captain. An order from the Navy Department on 17 April 1863, at a time when uniforms were hard to acquire, required all officers to wear the prescribed uniform of their grade whenever on duty.[3] Regulations theretofore required wearing of uniform only while on watch in port in good weather; at other times the officer merely had to wear his rank insignia.[4] The Secretary's order had to be suspended until June, when enough cloth finally arrived to make its enforcement practicable.

Brass buttons with the raised letters CSN were sold to officers, and were transferred from one uniform to another. Overcoat buttons were without lettering. The *Alabama*'s officers had gold epaulettes purchased while awaiting delivery of their ship in England, but it is doubtful if these adornments were worn within the Confederacy.

---

3. *C. S. Navy Register 1864*, 84–85.
4. *C. S. Navy Regulations*, 99.

From the beginning of the war, it was evident that there would be a shortage of uniforms and shoes. The army seized the factories at Graniteville, South Carolina, with which the navy had contracts, and held the navy to small allotments of cloth. It was necessary to look abroad for supplies. James D. Bulloch's orders of 9 May 1861 directed him to buy outfits of blankets and clothing similar to those used by the British navy but without insignia.[5] Similar purchases were directed throughout the war, always with emphasis on urgency.[6] Some contracts were made in Richmond with representatives of foreign companies or with Confederates who wanted to buy for the government, but few deliveries were made.

Domestic naval agents purchased cloth on the open market or from auctions of goods which had run the blockade, and then supervised the manufacture of uniforms at Richmond, Savannah, and Mobile.[7] At first Paymaster De Bree and the commanders of some ships and stations objected to the lack of uniformity resulting from this system, but they finally concluded that varied apparel was better than none.[8]

An act of 30 April 1863 permitted price increases only fifty per cent above prices at the beginning of the war for clothing issued to sailors.[9] The temptation to speculate on clothing bought at bargain prices caused the Office of Provisions and Clothing to warn all commanding officers to be careful to keep sailors from disposing of their clothing.[10]

In the fall of 1864, the men of the James River squadron often had to stand watches barefoot on iron decks without peacoats or even blankets to wrap around themselves. Fires were not allowed, and there was no room for exercise.

Shoes were hard to get. Sailors were used to climbing rigging or working barefoot in sailing vessels, but shoes

---

5. *O.R.N.*, ser. 2, II, 65.
6. *Ibid.*, 86, 368, 372, 805.
7. *Ibid.*, 554.
8. John De Bree to W. W. Hunter, 3 November 1863, Hunter Collection, Tulane University.
9. *Digest*, 218.
10. *O.R.N.*, ser. 2, II, 555.

were a necessity on steam vessels. Fire and engine rooms were generally uninsulated; and, while the decks above them got unbearably hot, in winter the rest of the deck armor was often covered with a film of ice or sleet. In 1863 Paymaster Thomas R. Ware of the Mobile station manufactured canvas shoes which proved so serviceable that the Office of Provisions and Clothing sent his plans to other stations.[11]

11. *Ibid.*, 555.

15

The Office of Provisions and Clothing: Fiscal Matters

T H E Office of Provisions and Clothing was also responsible for pay and other fiscal matters. The pay table is
included in the Appendix. Two features not shown in the
table are noteworthy. First, in order to maintain the idea
of a strong currency and also in order to hold to service the
large proportion of foreign sailors who had shipped into
the cruisers, the pay of men serving abroad was in gold
rather than in the greatly inflated currency. Second, the
pay of seamen was left to presidential discretion; seamen
shipped for the cruisers were paid more than seamen at
home. Thus, a sailor on the *Alabama* got many times the
pay of a sailor abroad an ironclad at Charleston, Savannah,
or Richmond.

A man's pay account consisted of a record of the date
of his enlistment, its term, his advancement in grade, pay-
ments made to him, commutation of spirit ration, and pay
advances. This account, signed by the paymaster and the
sailor, went with the sailor when he was transferred, except when he went to a hospital and was expected to return
in a short time.[1] An officer's pay record included, in addition to the items given above, copies of his appointment or

---

1. *C. S. Navy Regulations*, 17.

commission, the date he reported for duty, and the date he entered on sea or shore duty. Monthly pay rolls containing the names and amounts due to both officers and men were presented to the captain for approval. The captain or squadron commander could direct that up to three months' pay be withheld in an effort to prevent desertion. A person in debt to the government was not to be paid, except that an officer in debt was allowed to receive pay for one ration.[2]

If a man died, his pay was not delivered to his administrator or executors until approval was received from the Treasury Department. The paymaster took charge of the deceased's personal effects and clothing and sold them at auction if he were in debt to the government; otherwise, he held them for the deceased's representatives.[3] Funeral expenses were borne by the government when sanctioned by the Secretary of the Navy or the commander-in-chief of a fleet.[4]

There was an allotment system for those who wished to send up to one half their salaries to a near relative, wife, or guardian, but the man had to reserve at least six dollars per month for himself.[5]

Naval agents furnished tickets for travel to sailors and to officers accompanying drafts of sailors. Officers travelling under orders on commercial transportation could do so at their own expense or could get an advance from the navy agent.[6] The act of 4 June 1864 allowed free transportation to officers and their baggage travelling under orders, plus ten dollars a day for expenses. Wounded or sick officers or men were allowed free transportation upon presentation of a certificate from a board of surgeons.[7]

A ship in home waters seldom had government funds except to meet its payroll. Most financial transactions were paper ones. A ship was given an allotment of funds divided

---

2. *Ibid.*, 75, 137.
3. *Ibid.*, 137.
4. *Ibid.*, 157.
5. *Ibid.*, 158.
6. *Ibid.*, 154–156.
7. *Digest*, 301.

into groups according to purpose, and the ship could requisition against her balance. Requisitions were submitted through the squadron commander or senior officer present and, upon approval, were turned over to the naval storehouse or navy agent for filling. The paymaster kept a ship's expense account which he submitted to the captain for examination and signature.

Ships abroad or preparing to go to sea were given either cruising funds in cash or letters of credit, usually on Fraser, Trenholm Company. This fund required accounting procedures of the same type as the expense account. The system operated well as long as the funds lasted, which was not long. Several times cruisers were delayed for a considerable time for lack of funds to pay port charges and bills. Considering the chaotic financial situation of the Confederacy, it was remarkable the navy accomplished as much as it did abroad.

After the Civil War, Confederate Navy veterans boasted that none of their number was accused of dishonesty in handling the enormous funds that passed through their hands. They overlooked one case—that of Paymaster's Clerk Brokenborough, who was accused of absconding with the money of CSS *Macon*'s paymaster. He was arrested in December 1864, but no record of legal proceedings against him has been found.[8] They might also have deplored the wild extravagance in vainly preparing New Orleans for invasion, though no dishonesty was charged.

Pay in the Confederate Navy, as in the army, was inadequate and frequently in arrears. As a result, families of servicemen often had insufficient funds to sustain themselves adequately.

---

8. Thomas W. Brent to W. W. Hunter, 29 December, 1864, Savannah Squadron Papers #1228, Emory Special Collections.

16

The Office of Medicine and Surgery

W. A. W. Spotswood, Surgeon in Charge: 1861–1865
C. N. Fennell, Chief Clerk: 1862–1865
Robert Lecky, Purveyor: Summer 1863–1865

T H E Office of Medicine and Surgery was responsible for all purchases of medicine and medical supplies for the navy and for such other duties pertaining to the medical department as the Secretary might direct.[1] The Surgeon saw to the health of the navy and supervised hospitals and medical officers generally.

The Surgeon in Charge, W. A. W. Spotswood, was a hearty six-footer, a veteran of over thirty years naval service, who in 1861 had only recently returned from the East Indies Squadron. He was the third senior surgeon in the Confederate Navy.

There were approximately eighty-nine medical officers: surgeons, passed assistant surgeons (after 21 April 1862), assistant surgeons, and assistant surgeons for the war (after 21 December 1861). All twenty-two surgeons and most of the passed assistant surgeons were former United States Navy officers. The surgeon's steward was a petty officer of high grade. Hospital nurse was a rating used in the navy, although nothing could be found as to the seniority or duties.[2]

---

1. *Digest*, 200.
2. Passed assistant surgeon R. R. Gibbs to W. W. Hunter, 13 April 1865, Savannah Squadron Papers #1324, Emory Special Collections.

Medical officers served aboard ship, on staffs, at naval stations, naval hospitals, in the shore batteries, in rendezvous, and in the field with marines. One doctor and one or two men comprised the medical complement of each of these commands except hospitals, which had larger staffs.

Naval hospitals were located in facilities formerly occupied by the United States Navy at Norfolk and Pensacola, and others were set up at Richmond, Charleston, Mobile, Savannah, and Wilmington. Doctors assigned to naval stations or ships near hospitals had additional duty in the hospitals.

One of the most important duties of medical officers was to keep healthy men well by insuring adequate diets and hygienic living conditions. From time to time, the surgeon in charge ordered boards of medical officers to inspect and report health conditions to him. He then made recommendations to the Secretary, the officer in charge of Provisions and Clothing, or the squadron or station commander. The reports were seriously considered and used as a basis for appropriate action.

The surgeons consistently defended the spirit ration as a medical measure, though sea officers commonly opposed it on disciplinary grounds and paymasters resisted it for economic reasons.

Normal routine for the care of the sick in the Confederate Navy was much like that previously followed in the United States Navy. Doctors were required to keep medical journals and submit them to the Office of Medicine and Surgery when directed. Officers who were chronically ill were given sick leave to recuperate at home and were required to report in to the Secretary of the Navy at stated intervals. A sailor with an ailment reported to his medical officer, who treated him and sent him back to duty if possible. If the man were seriously ill, either he was given a "sick ticket" which removed him from duty or he was sent to the hospital. Sick sailors were often discharged, and one of the problems was the lack of an adequate pension system for them such as they had enjoyed in the old navy. Ultimately the navy shared the invalid corps set up by the army. Disabled officers and men in this corps were mustered and examined at intervals, were required to serve in a limited duty status, and were given half pay. Late in the war, they were periodically permitted to draw government cloth to make uniforms.[3]

An important part of Surgeon Spotswood's Richmond office was the purveyor's department under Robert Lecky, a chemist and apothecary. Lecky and his two assistants acquired, concocted, and delivered their materials with a success and economy that were extremely gratifying to Spotswood. The manufactures included such items as sulfuric acid, opiates, and iodine, all of which Spotswood claimed to have produced at less than half the amount that would have been charged had they been bought through John Fraser and Company from England. Efforts were also made to import pharmaceuticals, and some few drugs were received. A particularly welcome cache was received with the capture of the Norfolk Navy Yard. The navy, unlike the army, did not suffer from lack of medicines.

Surgeons found conditions aboard the ironclads quite different from those that they had known on sea vessels in the old navy. Berthing spaces on the ironclads were so poorly ventilated as to be practically uninhabitable. Men off duty usually lived aboard the receiving ship or a tender. Unlike sailing vessels, the ironclads afforded little opportunity for strenuous outdoor exercise, and men became flabby and subject to pulmonary diseases when readiness requirements

---

3. *C. S. Navy Regulations*, 122–129; *C. S. Navy Register 1864*, 80–81.

forced them to remain aboard for extended periods. Anchorage in swamp areas, usually avoided in peacetime, brought on malaria and yellow fever. One benefit of the otherwise objectionable commando raids was that the men got exercise in the fresh air.

Confederate medical officers were perceptive of the problems of environment and of diet. They made timely, intelligent, and practical recommendations for improvements in the general health aspects of their duties. The Office of Medicine and Surgery issued its *Instructions for the Guidance of the Medical Officers of the Navy* (Richmond, 1864) which stressed diet, hospital routine, and similar matters.

The medical department of the navy performed its mission as well as knowledge, techniques, and supplies permitted. Acting assistant surgeon W. H. Pierson, United States Navy prisoner of the Confederate Navy, was encouraged to work in the Savannah naval hospital in 1864. He reported the hospital airy and comfortable, though devoid of luxuries. Patients, including prisoners, were given as good care as could be afforded in the blockaded country. They received better food, including tea and butter, than the surgeons' mess with whom Pierson ate.[4]

---

4. *O.R.N.*, ser. 1, XV, 482–485.

17

The Chief Constructor

The Chief Constructor
John L. Porter: April 1863–end of war

T H E Confederate States Navy did not assign specific responsibility for the construction, equipment, and repair
of ships and shore establishments until July 1863. The failure of the Southern navy to provide at its inception for
supervision of a shipbuilding, conversion, and purchasing
program is surprising. Secretary Mallory's first report to
the President, dated 26 April 1861, stated that it would be
his policy to buy ships, including ironclads, abroad rather
than try to build them at home, since twelve to eighteen
months would be required to build an ironclad in the Confederacy and such a ship would cost eighty per cent more if
built at home than if obtained abroad.[1] Adoption of this
policy did not remove the need of providing responsible
officers at the seat of government to review costs and approve
plans.

The initial personnel allocation of the navy did permit
the commissioning of as many naval constructors as were
needed.[2] A naval constructor for the Pensacola Navy Yard
was included in the expense estimates submitted by Mallory on 12 March 1861.[3] Owing to gunfire from Union-held

---

1. *O.R.N.*, ser. 2, II, 51.
2. *Digest*, 202.
3. *O.R.N.*, ser. 2, II, 48.

Fort Pickens, the Pensacola Navy Yard did not build any ships; but once the Norfolk Navy Yard fell to the Confederates, facilities were available for building, modifying, and repairing ships. John L. Porter, constructor at Pensacola prior to secession, became constructor at the Norfolk yard and at once became involved with salvaging and rebuilding the *Merrimack* into an ironclad. The success of this undertaking and Porter's service in the United States Navy resulted in his selection as the Secretary's technical adviser on ship construction. When Porter moved to the Rocketts yard near Richmond, he retained his position as adviser to the secretary.

When Mallory in 1863 requested the establishment of the office and title of chief naval constructor for the Confederate Navy, it was at the suggestion of Porter, who proposed the position and nominated himself to fill it.[4] On 30 April 1863, Congress authorized the President to appoint "one chief constructor in the navy, whose compensation shall be three thousand dollars per annum, and who shall perform such duties as may be directed by the Secretary of the Navy."[5] A Navy Department general order directed that all communications concerning construction and repair of vessels be addressed to the chief constructor.[6] He probably had part-time use of a Navy Department draftsman after congress established that position.[7] Two acting constructors, Joseph Pearce and William A. Graves, were also appointed.

Congressmen, generals, contractors, and naval officers submitted concepts, proposals, or plans to the Secretary. Some of the concepts were original, simple, and feasible. Others were impractical, complicated, or impossible. The Secretary was inexperienced, enthusiastic, and often gullible. The system of developing plans which ultimately came

---

4. *Ibid.*, 271–272.
5. *Digest*, 211.
6. *C. S. Navy Register 1864*, 87.
7. *Digest*, 200.

into being was never explained in writing but became fairly standard. The chief constructor was responsible for the hull form of the ship, steering apparatus, decks, interior furnishings, small boats, and general supervision of construction. The engineer-in-chief was responsible for propulsion engines and boilers. Guns, armor, ammunition storage, navigational instruments, and protection against torpedoes were planned by the Office of Ordnance and Hydrography. The Office of Orders and Detail saw to anchor gear, coal and water storage, sails, and masts. The Secretary of the Navy was the coordinator and final arbiter. He was, unfortunately, without a disinterested assistant such as U. S. Secretary of Navy Gideon Welles had in Assistant Secretary of Navy Gustavus Fox, to whom he could assign the authority to settle controversies. Mallory had to do the job himself, and he lacked the necessary knowledge and decisiveness.

John L. Porter's background as a naval constructor was unimpressive, but he appears to have been the only experienced constructor available.[8] As far back as 1846 he had been involved in experiments with ironclad vessels. He had failed an examination in 1847 for appointment as a constructor in the United States Navy, but succeeded in securing appointment by 1857. In 1860 Porter was tried for gross neglect of duty before a court-martial in connection with the construction of USS *Seminole* but was exonerated.[9]

Porter's claim to fame is his part in the reconstruction of the *Merrimack*. Although controversy raged for thirty years after the Civil War as to who was primarily responsible for the concept of the ship (John M. Brooke's supporters seem to have the best case), there is no doubt that Porter had an important part in shaping the plans finally adopted. It was Porter who drew these plans and Porter who had charge of the modification of the hull, while Chief Engineer Wil-

---

8. *U. S. Navy Register 1860*, 97.
9. James P. Baxter, *The Introduction of the Ironclad Warship* (Cambridge, Mass., 1933), 226.

liam P. Williamson suggested the use of the salvaged *Merri-mack*, Brooke laid out the armor, and Catesby ap R. Jones placed the guns.[10] The success of the *Merrimack* reflects credit on all concerned.

However there are three details which reflect adversely on Porter's judgment and skill as constructor. The first is that he negligently omitted some weights from his calculations as to the final draft of the *Merrimack* so that several hundred tons of lead ballast had to be taken aboard in order to get her armor plate under the water. The second had to do with the destruction of the *Merrimack* by Commodore Josiah Tattnall on May 11, 1862. When it became evident that Norfolk must be abandoned, Tattnall tried to ascertain the least draft at which the *Merrimack* could retain stability, so as to allow her to retreat up the James River. In reply to a written inquiry and without calculations or references to files, Chief Constructor Porter gave an offhand answer: "Seventeen feet." Every possible weight was removed but still she drew eighteen feet, too much to go upriver or over the bar to sea. An armorless section above her waterline was exposed, leaving her vitals unprotected. She could no longer remain in Norfolk, could not flee, and could not fight. Her captain was left with no option except to destroy her. The loss was not entirely Porter's fault, but better information from him would have left Tattnall the alternative of fighting. The third was the fact that in 1864 Porter gave the army erroneous information as to the drafts of the James River Squadron vessels when the Confederate Navy was preparing to make a dash at the Federals downriver.[11]

After a plan for building a ship or reconstructing a ship within the Confederacy had been accepted by the Secretary of the Navy, either a contract was given to a civilian

---

10. *O.R.N.*, ser. 2, I, 783–788; II, 174–176; Robert Underwood Johnson and Clarence Clough Buel, eds., *Battles and Leaders of the Civil War* (New York, 1887) I, 717; John M. Brooke, "The *Virginia* or *Merrimack*, Her Real Projector," The Southern Historical Society *Papers* IX: 3–34, January 1891.
11. *O.R.N.*, ser. 1, VII, 796; X, 646.

concern or else a naval officer or civilian working for the navy was assigned the duty of coordinating the construction. Contracts were negotiated, but competitive bidding does not seem to have taken place.

The Navy Department furnished a naval constructor or other naval officer acting in this capacity to both private or public builders to act as the government's representative and inspector. In public contracts, the naval constructor was responsible for assembling materials, and a paymaster paid bills as directed by him. A private contractor was paid portions of the contract price at intervals based on the progress of construction. The commandant of the station in whose area the ship was built was expected to keep himself and the Secretary informed as to the progress of building. He was not supposed to direct changes in plans, although he might make suggestions to the Secretary, who alone had legal authority over the builder. The chief constructor made periodic visits to building yards, reporting progress to the Secretary. In the last few weeks before commissioning, the crew was assembled by the commandant and the officers ordered to duty by the Secretary through the Office of Orders and Detail. The prospective commanding officer was without legal authority over the ship until she was placed in commission, although he could report unsatisfactory work or progress to the commandant or to the Secretary.

In the case of ships built abroad, Confederate States naval representatives had almost complete authority, within the bounds of appropriations, the confidence of European constructors in the ability of the Confederate States to pay, and the delicacy of the diplomatic situation. Owing to the necessity for secrecy, Confederate supervision of construction in Europe was impracticable. Very detailed plans and contracts had to be made with shipbuilders of high repute.

Thus, experienced European shipyards and workmen were expected to be furnished with detailed and accurate plans, while inexperienced domestic constructors were to have comparatively little guidance in writing.

In operation, the system was more complicated. A proposal to build a ship might be the result of someone's inventive mind, the discovery of an intact steam engine, fear of enemy attack, or the existence of an unexpended appropriation. Usually there was a congressman behind the project. Often a contractor would send Mallory an outline drawing, and Mallory would direct the Constructor and the Engineer in Chief to prepare a plan and a model. Mallory kept the models in his office. Sometimes it was necessary for the Navy Department to send an officer or a civilian out to the area in which it was desired to build a ship, with instructions to locate a builder or to start construction himself. Unless the builder already had a shipyard (and there were few yards in the South) it was necessary for the builder to locate a large, clear, level area on firm ground near water deep enough to permit launching, close to rail transportation, and, if possible, adjacent to an industrial center with a large supply of trained labor.

With the exception of the Norfolk Navy Yard, none of the southern shipyards kept a large force of permanent laborers. Cut-throat competition for labor often resulted when two or more contracts for naval vessels were let in the same area. Sometimes workers struck for higher wages or shorter hours. Strikes delayed for several days work on the *Louisiana* and *Mississippi* on the eve of the fall of New Orleans. Workers in Mobile went on strike when Captain Ebenezer Farrand ordered the work day increased from nine hours to ten. Secretary Mallory urged night and Sunday work. Builders generally opposed the idea on account of fire hazard and also the lack of an adequate number of supervisors. However, workers often went on shifts in the shops in order to expedite construction. With workmen extremely scarce everywhere in the South, it became necessary to ask for details from the army and to recruit artisans from abroad. Another expedient was the hiring of Negroes, though navy regulations forbade the employment of slaves in any capacity without permission of the Navy Department. Shop practices and ship design were simplified as far as possible to permit inexperienced labor and unseasoned wood to be used.

The Confederacy had more than enough timber to meet its shipbuilding needs, but it lacked adequate facilities for transporting lumber to shipyards. Assembly of the millions of board feet required for an ironclad (the Confederate ironclad *Louisiana* required two million)[12] was a task of massive proportions, and construction was sometimes delayed by tardy deliveries. The naval ropewalk furnished adequate amounts of cordage and rigging lines.

The two material items which caused the most concern were iron and propulsion machinery. Most of the iron mining, smelting, and rolling facilities in the Confederacy lay along the Tennessee and Ohio Rivers and were soon behind Union lines. New mines and smelters had to be developed (mostly in Alabama), and rolling mills built (principally at Atlanta), to augment the heavily-committed Tredegar Iron Works in Richmond. The Navy Department sought allocations of new iron from the Army's Nitre and Mining Bureau but the contractors and constructors always had to push hard to get or augment their allocation. Commander James W. Cooke, who was ordered to take over the construction of the *Albemarle* on the Roanoke River after the private contractor had failed to complete the job, became known as

12. *O.R.N.*, ser. 2, I, 758.

the "Ironmonger Captain" because of his persistence in gathering scrap iron. Some plate was sent from England.

The Navy Department claimed engines from wrecked ships all over the Confederacy, and often parts of several ships were used to equip one vessel. Sometimes a ship was laid down without any idea of the characteristics of her engines or even their dimensions. Commander James D. Bulloch bought a number of engines and boilers in England and sent them through the blockade. The larger engines thus acquired should have been a great asset, but it is unknown whether any of them arrived in time to be put in service.[13]

It was the responsibility of the Office of Ordnance and Hydrography to order guns and ammunition to the ships, but sometimes the builder of a ship or the commandant of the station had to take the initiative. For instance, the guns for the New Orleans ironclads were so delayed in April 1862 by army requirements after the battle of Shiloh that an officer had to be sent to accompany the weapons to New Orleans. In 1864, only two months before one of Buchanan's ironclads was scheduled to be completed, neither he nor Commander Catesby ap R. Jones, who had to make the guns, knew what kind they were to be.

If good plans, adequate labor, appropriate material, and sufficient time were available, building an ironclad was fairly simple. Heavy wooden ways were built on a bank gently sloping down into the water. A keel was laid so that the stern piece was just above the high water mark, and ribs were built out from the keel. If the engines, boilers, and shafts were available they were usually installed while the ship was on the ways; otherwise, the shaft exit was sealed off and a watertight box (cofferdam) was built over the stern in order to allow underwater work to resume after launching.

---

13. *Ibid.*, II, 184.

Apparently no ceremony accompanied launchings. At the right moment (high water, about to start falling) wedges were knocked loose from the keel and the vessel was supposed to slide smoothly into the water. The *Mississippi* was so hard to launch that three tugs which took her in tow failed to get her off. Investigation revealed that through accident or the work of saboteurs a wooden dowel pin had been driven between the ship's bottom and the dry dock ways.[14] A similar incident occurred in launching the floating battery *Georgia*; she was said to have had a plank from the ways stuck to her bottom to the end of her days.[15]

After a vessel was in the water, her machinery was completed, armor was installed, and the gun ports were adjusted to whatever guns and gun carriages were available when the ship was ready. The ship had to be heeled over on one side in order to facilitate laying the armor on the opposite side, and then the process reversed to complete the job. The Confederate Navy never adequately solved the problem of laying out the guns in such a manner that the crews would be well protected, and the guns given space for a wide and high angle of fire. The Office of Ordnance and Hydrography apparently lacked jurisdiction in the matter and the chief constructor proved unequal to the task.

The lack of a completely integrated ship design is seen not only in the case of ordnance, but in that of the engines as well. Under the best of conditions, a ship is a complex compromise of incompatible requirements. New developments in ordnance made the use of armor essential. Armor meant weight, and weight called for an increase in size. Size could be attained by designing a deep draft vessel, which the shallow rivers and flat coastline would not permit, or by designing longer or wider ships. Broad, long ships needed more armor to protect the larger area, strong engines to

14. *Ibid.*, I, 537.
15. *Ibid.*, ser. 1, XIII, 776.

move them, and enormous rudders for steering. Heavy armor was thick and it had to be installed at an angle to keep it from sliding off and also make it less vulnerable to hostile fire. This made gun ports excessively large, weakened the hull, and narrowed the angle of fire. The Union navy adopted the turret system in which the entire vessel was built to house a few big guns. Construction so oriented was economical of space and weight, but its use would have required skill and machinery far beyond what was available to the Confederacy.

Although it was impracticable for the Confederacy to build power-driven revolving gun turrets, Southern designers would have been wise to use the most critical factor in construction and operation as the starting point for their plans. The main propulsion machinery was almost always the most troublesome item in Confederate warships.[16] Since this machinery had to be improvised from whatever pieces could be scavenged from other vessels or built at Tredegar or Columbus, the South's only adequate engine plants, it is evident that all else (except draft) should have adapted to the size, shape, and general characteristics of available engines. The hull form, guns, armor, control apparatus, living areas, and storage spaces should then have been laid out to conform to engineering requirements. In other words, the draft and the engineering arrangements should have been treated as constants, with other characteristics as variables.

Another failure in design was that of steering gear. In wooden ships, wheel ropes ran along below deck to the rudder area with chains standing ready to be rigged on deck if the ropes burned or were broken. With the coming of the ironclad, a problem arose of piercing the armor for ropes

---

16. For discussion of this problem see Chapter 18.

and chain. Designers at first attempted to keep steering controls inside the armor but this took up so much inside space that they resorted to running them along deck. A few days before the battle of Mobile Bay Admiral Buchanan ordered the constructor to put an "iron tunnel-way" over the *Tennessee*'s exposed rudder controls. One of the first hits from the Union gunfire bent this tunnel so badly that the steering gear was jammed and the ship was unmanageable for the remainder of the action.

Still another defect of Confederate naval ship design was that almost all the ironclads drew too much water. Union ships, except those on the Mississippi system, had to have deep draft to give them stability for the ocean voyages they must complete in order to get in the fight. This was not so for the Confederacy, for Southern ships, except the cruisers, were restricted largely to shallow water. As stated above, ship design requires much compromise. One thing which could not be sacrificed in the Confederacy was shallow draft. Southern ships should have been designed with an extremely careful eye on draft. A ruthless reduction of weight should have been enforced including decrease of stores allowances to a few days instead of a month's supply. It was highly important that information on the ship's draft be constantly known; yet the Secretary and Porter gave it slight concern, and both were sometimes uninformed.

In execution of shipbuilding plans as drawn, the Confederate Navy also failed in several ways. For one thing, ship construction almost always took more time than expected. Some delays were avoidable, but no one seemed to foresee chronic bottlenecks until too late to remedy them. Then the Secretary habitually took personal, but ineffectual, charge of breaking the bottlenecks to the detriment of his other duties. There should have been some sort of system and an officer responsible for scheduling material and for discovering and reporting what items were going to be late.

As was pointed out in Chapter Four, there was a general lack of mechanics for naval construction, and the Secretary's half-hearted efforts failed to secure the cooperation of the army in getting detailed men or exempt artisans.

Approximately twenty-one ironclads (the exact number depends upon the definition of the word "ironclad") were built or converted within the Confederacy, a tremendous feat considering the lack of an industrial economy in the pre-war South.

18

The Engineer in Chief

Engineer in Chief
>Chief Engineer William P. Williamson: 21 April 1862–
end of war

LIKE the position of chief constructor, that of engineer in chief was not initially established by law, but came into existence by necessity and took on added functions as time went on. Its task was the design, acquisition, installation, operation, and maintenance of power machinery afloat and ashore.

Since engineering was still a comparatively new field in the navy, the status of engineers was not clearly defined in the laws and customs carried over from the old service. In some respects, as in succession to command afloat and in matters of discipline and rank, engineers were similar to medical officers, paymasters, or constructors. In others, like military command of men in battle and administrative duties ashore and afloat, they were similar to sea officers.

In addition to the engineer in chief, there was one grade of commissioned officer: chief engineer; and three grades of warrant officer: first, second, and third assistant engineer. All eight of the chief engineers originally appointed (including Williamson) were former officers of the

United States Navy with from seven to eighteen years service. The four officers subsequently promoted to chief engineer (except for James H. Tomb, promoted for gallantry in action) were likewise officers of the old navy. A formal examination was required for eligibility before promotion to chief engineer.

Assistant engineers, being warrant officers, could be appointed by the Secretary of the Navy or be given acting appointments by specifically authorized officers, subject to the Secretary's approval. It was not unusual for the engineers of the Confederate cruisers to be citizens of European countries (especially Great Britain) or to be engineers hired for the voyage. This was unsatisfactory from a military point of view and by 1864 strong efforts were made to ensure that at least one of the officers in the engineering department, preferably the senior, be a member of the regularly established navy and a citizen of one of the Confederate states.[1] A board of chief engineers headed by Michael Quinn, next senior after Williamson, was appointed by Mallory in the summer of 1864 to examine assistant engineers for promotion.[2]

In addition to engineers appointed from civil life, it was common to promote experienced enlisted men to the junior ranks. There were no educational requirements for appointments; an experienced fireman barely able to read and write and totally deficient in the theoretical aspects of engineering was considered qualified for appointment as third assistant engineer, although not as second assistant.[3]

Enlisted grades in descending order of seniority were fireman first class, fireman second class, and coal heaver. These men received considerably higher pay than their opposite numbers in the deck force, more on account of the dangerous and unpleasant nature of their duties than be-

---

1. *O.R.N.*, ser. 2, II, 582.
2. S. S. Lee to W. W. Hunter, 24 August 1864, Savannah Squadron Papers #1003, Emory Special Collections.
3. L. Campbell to W. W. Hunter, 21 July 1864, Savannah Squadron Papers #922, Emory Special Collections.

cause of special skills or knowledge. If a man became incapable of performing his duties with the engines, his pay was temporarily reduced to that of the next junior grade. Men with experience in steamboats, locomotives, or sawmills often entered the navy as firemen; otherwise, engineers recruited their men from landsmen already aboard ship who volunteered for assignment as coal heavers.

At the beginning of the war, engineering officers served exclusively within their own branch either aboard ship or in the navy yards. As time went on, the special skills of the well-trained engineers in the South were increasingly in demand and chief engineers were to be found in command of or assigned to ordnance works as well. Major commands had chief engineers attached to their staffs, and at least one chief engineer was sent abroad to aid in procurement of engines. Chief engineers also served on trial boards for new or rebuilt ships and as examining boards for promotion of engineers. A few were in charge of the engineering departments of ships. The first, second, and third class engineers were almost all assigned to ships in their specialty.

Chief Engineer William P. Williamson was involved in the conversion of the *Merrimack* from frigate into ironclad; it was he who had suggested utilizing the hulk. Williamson had been on duty in the Norfolk Navy Yard since 1856, having been one of the first officers appointed in the United States Navy when the engineering branch was formed in 1842. Williamson's educational background is not known, but he apparently had little knowledge of theory or drafting. Nevertheless he was appointed engineer in chief of the Confederate Navy when that post was established on 21 April 1862.

The office of the engineer in chief performed two main functions. It furnished engineering designs for new ships or major alterations of old ships and it conducted or supervised trials and inspections. It issued no operating instructions, safety regulations, or compilations of engineering data. It instituted no training program for officers or men.

Work emanating from the office of the chief engineer left much to be desired. When Mallory decided to accept Commander Bulloch's suggestion that prefabricated boilers, engines, and auxiliary machinery be sent from Europe for installation in hulls under construction in the Confederacy, grave errors were discovered in the plans drawn up in the office of the engineer in chief. The drawings sent abroad were often marred by inconsistencies, omissions, and imprecise tracings. With mail taking one to three months each way across the Atlantic, time to rectify errors was prohibitively great.[4]

At home several ships were designed with boilers incapable of producing as much steam as the engines required to develop full power. The great ironclad *Louisiana* built in New Orleans in 1861–62 had the monstrously impractical design feature of two paddles one in front of the other, midway between stem and stern along the fore and aft centerline of the ship. The *Mississippi*, under construction in New Orleans at the same time, had inadequate boiler power for the engines. It was necessary to add eight more boilers and lengthen the ship by twenty feet to accommodate them. This greatly increased cost and decreased already limited maneuverability to almost nothing; it also took time, and this the hard pressed Confederacy could not spare.

Plans for small forty- to fifty-foot steamboats to be used as torpedo vessels were also defective in engineering design. The layout called for boilers twenty feet long, to be placed parallel with the keels in order to make the little ships nar-

---

4. *O.R.N.*, ser. 2, II, 688, 724, 790.

row-beamed. The door on the boiler opened to the side. This position made it impossible to insert the long slice bar which was needed to break clinkers and to spread fires to the back of the fire box. Also, the side door was so large that it could not be fully opened to allow the coal heaver to get his shovel properly into the furnace.[5] The fiasco of impossible-to-fire boilers, added to deficiencies previously demonstrated, brought Mallory in December 1864 to the realization that his engineer in chief was unsatisfactory; but he failed to replace him.[6]

The faulty design of ship engineering plants may be partially extenuated by the dearth of competent naval architects and draftsmen, but the failure of the engineer in chief to issue adequate operating instructions, safety precautions, and compilations of engineering data is inexcusable. A law of 1850 had given specific and fairly detailed instructions for passenger boats, particularly on high pressure river vessels. It should have taken comparatively little work to adapt these or similar rules to Confederate naval use. Three main types of engineering malfunctions occurred on Confederate vessels, some of which were costly in human lives; yet no lessons seem to have been learned from them and no action seems to have been taken to guide the inexperienced engineers aboard ship. A boiler explosion which caused the worst engineering disaster of the war occurred aboard the CSS *Chattahoochee* on the river of the same name, about fifty miles below Columbus, Georgia. The fireman on watch let the water level in his boiler fall. The pilot, who had no business being in the engine room, opened the valve which admitted water to the empty boiler. The sudden rush of cold water into the red hot boiler caused it to flash into steam at terriffic pressure. The boiler blew up, killing six

---

5. *Ibid.*, 682–684.
6. *Ibid.*, 779.

officers and twelve men, wounding many others, and plac-
ing the mangled ship out of service for a year.[7] No warning
was issued to other ships; no investigation was made; no
steps were taken to prevent recurrences.

The second type of engineering malfunction resulted
from a boiler "salting up"; that is, by the residual salts in
impure boiler water baking onto and insulating boiler
tubes with consequent loss of efficiency and sometimes
burned tubes. Modern practice calls for draining sludge
concentrations out of trycocks on the bottom of boilers, and
also for mechanical cleaning at stated intervals. These two
means of removing salts were known before the Civil War,
and were simple to design into a boiler and to manipulate.
Nevertheless, no instructions were issued beyond the vague
admonition in Navy Regulations for commanding officers to
allow firemen time to remove incrustations and deposits.[8]

The third most usual type of malfunction was the
breakdown caused by pushing the plant beyond its capacity,
a natural result of enthusiasm combined with inexperience.
The case of the ironclad *Arkansas* is the most dramatic example of uninformed overenthusiasm. The ship was a new
one, built up the Yazoo from Vicksburg by John T. Shirley
with the aid of the indomitable drive of Lieutenant Isaac
Brown and the technical skill of First Assistant Engineer
George W. City. The ship made a spectacular dash through
two Union fleets with City carefully nursing his engines
and Brown never requiring more than City thought advis-
able. The ship was badly cut up, Brown was wounded, and
City became ill.

With these key officers absent and because of a military
emergency downstream, the executive officer was prevailed
upon to get his ship underway without a single regularly
assigned engineering officer aboard. An army lieutenant

7. *Ibid.*, ser. 1, XVII, 868–874.
8. *C. S. Navy Regulations*, 84.

with experience running sawmills volunteered to act as engineer officer. Time was short; so the substitute engineer pushed his plant harder than City had ever permitted. A crank pin broke and the *Arkansas* lost time making emergency repairs; the lieutenant tried to make up the time by over-taxing the engine. There was a complete breakdown in the face of overwhelming enemy force, and the ship was destroyed without compensatory damage to the enemy.[9] The lesson seemed clear: a machine's proper operating capacity should have been determined, published, and not exceeded except by the most skilled persons and then only in the direct emergency. Yet not a word of caution about this type of danger has been found in Confederate sources beyond an admonition in Navy Regulations to conduct trials to establish fuel consumption rates.[10] The Offices of Ordnance and Hydrography, and Medicine and Surgery did not hesitate to issue instructions within their fields of cognizance, and the Engineer in Chief should have followed their examples.

It is not fair to compare Confederate operating naval engineers with their opponents. The South had furnished relatively few engineering officers in the old navy (thirty-two of the 174 in the 1860 register as compared to almost half the other officers of the navy) and very few sailors.[11] The proportion of civilian engineers was at least ten to one in favor of the Yankees. Similar proportions among the rest of the sailors were not as important since the inshore steamship and gunnery of the Civil War was so different from the old seagoing or riverboat ways. The Confederate Navy was severely handicapped by lack of engineers, and the deficiency became more common with the passing of time. As the war continued, more and more improvisations had to be made by less and less experienced engineers. Engineering deficiencies cost the Confederate Navy more op-

9. *O.R.N.*, ser. 1, XIX, 130.
10. *C. S. Navy Regulations*, 84.
11. *U. S. Navy Register 1860*, 88–95.

portunities and lost it more ships than any other cause except grounding; yet the Confederacy made no effort to educate engineers.

On the brighter side were the efforts of the Naval Works at Columbus, Georgia. Under the direction of Chief Engineer Warner, this station built at least eleven large engines and boilers for six steam vessels, repaired others, and made spare parts for many more. The Richmond works produced at least six engines for two ships.[12] The Charlotte Naval Works, mostly under Chief Engineer Henry A. Ramsey, had the only large forges in the Confederacy after Norfolk was lost. One of these forges, a Nasmith brought in from England through the blockade, made the only heavy shafts and certain other large parts which the Confederacy could produce. The ingenuity and resourcefulness of these works led to most of the engineering success experienced by the Confederate Navy. The navy could be proud that it had built more than seventeen large engines when none had been produced in the South before the war.

The senior officer of the engineering branch aboard ship was called chief engineer, whether his rank was chief engineer or first, second, or third assistant engineer. He was entitled to mess in the wardroom regardless of his rank. The chief engineer stood no watch, but was responsible for his engines at all times.

The chief engineer on a ship was supreme within his area, having far more authority over his men than did the lieutenants. There were occasional disputes over rank between executive officers and the engineers. The chief engineer had to make inspections at least daily, inspect and sign an engineering log, and hand it daily to the commanding officer, who signed it monthly. Daily and upon entering

---

12. *O.R.N.*, ser. 2, II, 251–253.

port, the chief engineer was expected to inspect his machinery, reporting possible repairs and their duration to the commanding officer.[13]

Underway, the assistant engineers were divided into watches, and one assistant engineer had to be aboard at all times in port. The engineer of the watch saw to the safe operation of the plant, keeping the officer of the deck informed of its status by means of hourly reports and also entering events of the watch in the engineering log.

Firemen and coal heavers were divided into watches and assigned duties in accordance with their experience and the needs of the ship. Men wishing to ship as firemen were supposed to be examined by a board of one or more engineers who were required to ascertain the candidates' abilities to manage fires with different kinds of fuel (not only anthracite and bituminous coal and various kinds of wood were used but also lard or bacon on occasion for quick heat) and to use smithy tools in the repair and maintenance of machinery and boilers.[14] They were supposed to be instructed in handling the engines without supervision, in case the watch officer was disabled.[15]

The complement of engineers varied but averaged about ten per cent of the men embarked; that is, from ten to twenty, divided about equally among the three ratings. There were usually a minimum of three watch officers in addition to the chief engineer. One to three junior engineers sometimes were embarked for instruction.

The engines in the ironclads were usually low pressure, less than fifty pounds per square inch, although some former western riverboat or sawmill engines of high pressure, 150 pounds per square inch, were used. Fifty to two hundred horsepower were generated, driving one to three

13. *C. S. Navy Regulations*, 118–120.
14. *U. S. Navy Register 1860*, 151–152.
15. *C. S. Navy Regulations*, 121.

propellers. A few paddle wheel warships were used by river forces, but it was generally easier to convert paddle wheelers to propeller ships than it was to give the paddles adequate protection. The average ironclad had two to four boilers of the fire tube type; that is, the fire passed through tubes submerged in the water drum. It was usually not possible to cross-connect the plant; the steam from a given boiler could be delivered only to its own engine. In some cases, all boilers gave steam to all engines and it was impossible to run with one engine crippled, unless the engines were stopped and the disabled unit disconnected. Even then great bellows of steam would be wasted, since there was no valve to be closed to isolate the trouble. This was one of the bad features of the *Merrimack*.

It was preferable to use anthracite because it gave a hot, even flame and comparatively little smoke. North Carolina coal was looked upon as almost worthless, but better than the wood which often had to be used in action and almost always when fires were banked in port.

Distilled water was not available for use in boilers but ships did attempt to obtain clear water from shoreside when possible. Some ships tried to condense exhaust steam in tanks. This had its hazards: Raphael Semmes claimed that heat from condensing tanks caused his powder magazines in the next compartment to become so hot that the *Alabama*'s powder deteriorated.

One item which Confederate naval engineers particularly sought when a prize was taken was sperm oil, which was used to lubricate machinery and for lighting. This commodity became very scarce.

An odd item found in enginerooms was oatmeal. It was introduced into the boilers in small quantities to prevent the water from foaming or priming (carrying over with the steam) as boiler water got more saline.[16]

Repairs were usually attempted on board by the ship's crew, except for major jobs such as replacing cracked or broken cylinders, valves, or shafts. Cylinders and valves were generally replaced by the Naval Works at Columbus and shafts by the Charlotte Works. Much scavenging occurred and it was not at all unusual for a vital part to be removed from one ship in order to allow a more important vessel to operate.

Engineering was one of the Confederate Navy's greatest weaknesses. Exceptions to the general rule were the marvelous improvisations on the part of many operating engineers and some outstanding achievements of the Columbus and Charlotte Works. Chiefly responsible for the generally poor performance in engineering was the Richmond office, which failed to train or recruit more engineers, provide adequate designs to domestic builders and foreign contractors, and furnish mature, helpful guidance for subordinates.

---

16. *C. S. Navy Regulations*, 89.

19

The Marine Corps

Commandant
Colonel Lloyd J. Beall: entire war

THE Confederate Marine Corps was organized so that the navy might have a small military force to protect its ships and stations from external attack or internal mutiny, and to make small-scale amphibious or boarding attacks.

The corps approximated an infantry regiment in size and composition, but with additional administrative and logistic sections. The commandant was a colonel and his assistant a lieutenant colonel. A paymaster, an adjutant, a major, a sergeant major, a quartermaster sergeant, and two clerks were also at the headquarters, 115 Maine Street, Richmond.[1]

The commandant came directly under the Secretary of the Navy and in that official's name issued orders concerning the Marine Corps to naval officers. The Secretary issued orders transferring companies from one command to another.

The paymaster (a former United States Navy purser) was bonded and charged with disbursing duties including periodic payment of troops. The quartermaster was respon-

---

1. *C. S. Navy Register 1864*, 34; Henry Graves to Mother, 20 August 1862, typescript, Georgia Department of Archives and History.

sible for commissary, clothing, and ordnance matters. The adjutant and inspector was aide, office manager, and administrator for the commandant.[2]

Field organization consisted of six to ten companies of a hundred privates and their officers, non-commissioned officers, and musicians. The original complement was six companies, but before these could be formed the number was raised to ten.[3] Each company was allowed a captain, first lieutenant, second lieutenant, two sergeants, two corporals, a fifer, and a drummer.

The company was an administrative unit from which guard units of six to twenty men were ordered to ships, naval stations, or to special duty. Since it was desirable to send an officer to command each detachment, the commandant obtained allotments of an additional second lieutenant to each company.[4]

Colonel Beall had served thirty years in the United States Army. His assistant, Lieutenant Colonel Henry B. Tyler, was formerly adjutant and inspector of the United States Marine Corps. Most officers of the rank of captain and above were former United States marine officers. Examinations for appointment to the rank of second lieutenant were given several times a year, as the need arose.

In early 1861, recruiting officers in New Orleans and Montgomery began enlisting men for the marines.[5] A hundred former United States marines are said to have enlisted in Richmond in May 1861.[6] After conscription began, recruits were obtained by sending marine officers to army camps of instruction, with authority of the War Department to enlist a stated number of men. The cruisers enlisted their own men. Most of the enlisted marines stationed in the Confederacy were of Irish origin, while those at sea were Germans.[7]

---

2. *O.R.N.*, ser. 2, II, 116.
3. *Ibid.*, 45, 251.
4. *Ibid.*, 53.
5. Four years, later reduced to three years or the war. *O.R.N.*, ser. 2, II, 154, 321.
6. Scharf, 770.
7. *O.R.N.*, ser. 1, I, 730; *Ibid.*, ser. 2, I, 313–316.

The first Marine Corps companies were formed at Pensacola and served under General Braxton Bragg. One by one companies were sent out until naval stations at Mobile, Savannah, Charleston, Wilmington, Richmond, and Camp Beall on Drewry's Bluff each had a company or more. These companies furnished guard detachments ashore, provosts for courts-martial, commando forces, and units for ships. Marines stationed on ships acted as gun crews or sharpshooters under their own officers. Sometimes they went out in picketboats as riflemen, and occasionally they landed to clear the riverbank of snipers or mine-tending groups.

At Drewry's Bluff, marines acted as guards, sharpshooters, skirmishers, and gun crews. By 1864, many of the navy gun crews had been withdrawn to the ships, and Major George H. Terrett, who commanded most of the Confederate marines, became commander of the battery there.[8]

The maximum strength of the Confederate Marine Corps (30 September 1864) was 571, including five officers and sixty-two men in enemy hands.[9] Companies were consolidated as they lost strength.

The Confederate Marine Corps had a disproportionately large administrative force for its size. It required its own uniforms, separate treatment afloat, and special orders ashore. There was a real need for the guard service that it performed at shore stations and even on board ship, particularly in the cruisers with their large proportion of unreliable and unruly foreigners, but its record with not without blemish.

Marines had many desertions and several near mutinies. Their officers were given to duels, courts-martial, and bickering over rank among themselves. It is doubtful that the service rendered by the marines as a separate unit war-

---

8. *Ibid.*, II, 747.
9. *Ibid.*, 749.

ranted the administrative manpower waste and the expense inherent in the special status and treatment necessary for a small organization.

20

Confederate Naval Administration In Europe

Commander James D. Bulloch: 9 May 1861–end of war
Commander James H. North: 17 May 1861–end of war
Commander George T. Sinclair: 7 May 1862–28 February 1865
Commander Matthew F. Maury: 20 September 1862–end of war
Flag Officer Samuel Barron: 29 August 1863–1 March 1865
Lieutenant William H. Murdaugh: January 1864–end of war

WITH the outbreak of the war between the United States and the Confederacy, it was at once evident that Southern industry was too primitive and slow to manufacture the complicated machinery and arms required for modern war. Even more than their Revolutionary War forebears, the Confederates were dependent upon European help; and, only a few weeks after war started, military and naval purchasing missions were sent abroad. At the same time and throughout the war, unofficial, sometimes unauthorized, private parties were also in Europe attempting to make contracts with various builders or manufacturers to deliver items to the Confederacy on terms which would allow them to make a tidy profit for themselves without risking any of their own money. It was not at all infrequent that two or more groups would be negotiating for the same ship or article, thus boosting the cost to the Confederacy.

The first, best-known, and most successful navy representative was James D. Bulloch. Born in 1823, Bulloch had served in the United States Navy from 1839 to about 1851 when he resigned to command mail steamers in which he continued to go to sea until after his state, Georgia, seceded. Sent abroad as a civilian on 9 May 1861, Bulloch was commissioned a commander for the war on 22 January 1862. Bulloch was the only officer not a regular in the United States Navy at the outset of the war to rise to the rank of commander in the Confederate Navy. Rightly realizing that his advanced rank would cause friction, he warned the Secretary of the Navy of the danger. A tactful, discreet, and clearheaded man, apparently honest, and a thorough seaman, Bulloch was ideal for his assignment. Except for one trip in 1861 to the Confederacy in command of the *Fingal* he spent the Civil War in Europe. He lived to see his half-sister's son, Theodore Roosevelt, elected vice-president of the United States in 1900.

The second naval representative to be sent abroad was Lieutenant James H. North, who had been a United States naval officer for ten years before Bulloch entered. When Bulloch was appointed a commander senior to him, North became so jealous as to render cooperation between the two representatives for a time impossible. North became somewhat reconciled when Samuel Barron "came over" in 1863 and thereafter worked satisfactorily.

Samuel Barron, son of a United States navy captain and nephew of the duelist who killed Stephen Decatur, was appointed a midshipman in 1812 at the age of two, as a kind of pension for his dead father. Gideon Welles claimed that he detected and thwarted an attempt of Barron to insinuate himself into control of the United States Navy Department while Virginia was on the verge of secession.[1] Barron resigned three days after his state seceded and entered the Virginia Navy.

Barron became Virginia's Officer in Charge of Naval Detail and Equipment on 29 April 1861. When the Virginia Navy was incorporated in the navy of the Confederacy, he served briefly as head of the Office of Orders and Detail, then was placed in charge of the naval defenses of Virginia and North Carolina. Captured at Fort Hatteras after he had assumed personal command ashore, Barron remained a prisoner for eleven months. When he was exchanged in November 1862, he was given command of the James River Squadron, where he remained until shortly before his departure for Europe. Barron was a suave, courtly man of most ingratiating manner and persuasive personality. He was nicknamed the sailor diplomat, a title which he clearly deserved in Europe.

Of the other naval officers abroad on independent missions, Commander George T. Sinclair and Lieutenant William H. Murdaugh were both ordnance officers of considerable experience in the United States Navy and in the Confederate Navy. Sinclair had helped seize the tremendously valuable powder magazine at the Norfolk Navy Yard, and Murdaugh had been badly wounded while heroically engaged in the battle for Fort Hatteras.

James D. Bulloch's initial orders were issued on 9 May 1861, the day before the act authorizing his mission was passed by congress. He was instructed to proceed to England and buy or have built six moderately armed but unarmored, steam-powered, propeller driven vessels, the vessels to be

---

1. Howard K. Beale, ed., *Diary of Gideon Welles* (New York, 1960), I, 16–21.

delivered in southern ports. These ships were to be shallow draft, fast under sail or steam, and provisioned with six months' stores. They were obviously to be used as commerce raiders, with prize money to be held out as an inducement for British sailors to enlist.

For transportation to the Confederacy in one or more of these ships, Bulloch was ordered to buy a thousand each rifles and revolvers with a hundred rounds of fixed ammunition and five hundred caps per firearm, along with corresponding supplies of bullets, molds, and spare parts. He was also to buy cutlasses, pyrotechnics for the ships, cannon, musket powder, and a thousand outfits each of navy and marine clothing. His instructions directed him to pay for these items in whole or in part with Confederate bonds. He was directed to consult with unnamed English commercial houses (Fraser, Trenholm and Company was apparently one of them) and with Confederate Army agents. The secret legislation authorizing his mission and appropriating a million dollars for its execution was approved by the President on 10 May 1861. Bulloch was assigned Paymaster's Clerk Clarence R. Yonge, Master's Mate (later Lieutenant) John Low, Lieutenant William F. Carter, and a secretary, M. P. Robertson. Still others from time to time worked out of his office.[2]

Shortly after Bulloch's appointment, a mission headed by Lieutenant James H. North was sent abroad to build if possible, otherwise to purchase, one or two war steamers of the most modern design with powerful armament and fully equipped for service. Mallory supported his request to congress for passage of the act to buy these war steamers with his famous and prophetic plea for ironclads. Two million dollars was appropriated for this purpose.

Mallory's orders to North are dated 17 May 1861. The

---

2. *O.R.N.*, ser. 2, II, 64–65, 83, 715, 782.

style and organization of the letters to Bulloch and North are so different that it is difficult to believe that they are of the same authorship; it seems likely that each officer drafted his own instructions and then went over them with the Secretary, who gave them to a clerk for copying. Bulloch's letter is straight to the point, but North's rambles considerably without coming to much of a conclusion, and is a little pompous.

Mallory wanted North to get a French ironclad of the recently completed *Gloire* class which the Secretary thought the best in the world. Relying upon the friendship and also the self-interest of the French in southern cotton, he hoped that the government would either agree to the sale of a ship directly to the Confederacy or at least permit its sale through an agent. If the purchase of a warship was not feasible, North was to arrange with the French government for construction of an ironclad. The construction was to be handled through French agents who were expected to keep secret the fact that they were acting for the Confederate States government, and were also expected to receive payment in Confederate bonds. Mallory authorizd a similar arrangement for a second vessel to be built in England. North was given considerable latitude as to armament but six to eight Armstrong 80-pounders, breech loading, were suggested. North was directed to arrange for coal, provisions, sails, ordnance, ordnance stores, and stores and outfits for a six months cruise. He was also directed to notify the Secretary when arrangements were expected to be completed so that formal contracts would be drawn up and officers and crew sent over. North was to confer, assist, and receive assistance from Bulloch and to keep the government informed of his movements and transactions. He was given no money and no assistants. Supplementary instructions told him to return in one of Bulloch's ships if his own mission failed.[3]

On 7 May 1862 Lieutenant George T. Sinclair was sent to England to buy and take command of a propeller-driven cruiser. His instructions were short and simple: he was to see Bulloch and find out what to do. Money for his project was furnished through Fraser, Trenholm and Company.[4]

In late 1862 Commander Matthew Fontaine Maury departed for Europe with instructions to purchase arms and equip vessels abroad. He was to pay for his purchases from the three million dollars in Confederate money unexpended out of four million dollars appropriated by an act of 6 October 1862, the remainder being turned over to Bulloch in the form of eight per cent treasury notes. Commander Hunter Davidson, Maury's relief in the mine warfare command in the Confederacy, came to Europe in the summer of 1864 and stayed several months. He and Maury both bought material for making, testing, and detonating mines; it is believed that Davidson worked for Maury.

Flag Officer Samuel Barron was sent abroad on 30 August 1863 with orders to take command of two ironclads Bulloch was expected to have ready for sea on about 1 October. He was directed not to interfere with Bulloch's arrangements, but to confer with him about shipping and embarking crews, including the offering of extra bounties if necessary. Barron was to inspect North's and Sinclair's ships and make reports and recommendations to the department as to each ship's character, fitness, state of completion, and prospect of getting to sea.

Barron was given authority to assign officers in the ships. It was Mallory's idea that the two ships should break the blockade at Charleston or Wilmington, also using Sinclair's or North's ships if available. Mallory favored what

---

3. *Ibid.*, 70–71, 81.
4. *Ibid.*, 191.

he called light infantry tactics to prevent the enemy from concentrating in one area. By this he meant that Barron's ships should steam separately but meet at a prestated time and place, defeat any enemy force in the area, establish a new rendezvous, and break up once more.

Lieutenant Murdaugh was sent abroad to buy ordnance equipment in January 1864. It may be that he was assigned to Bulloch after working under Barron for a time while awaiting assignment to a ship.

Chief Engineer Michael Quinn went over in November 1864 to inspect some engines being built by Bulloch; he assisted Bulloch in other matters in Europe.[5]

Paymaster Felix Senac, who was disbursing officer for the officers and men in Europe and Barron's sole office assistant, was assigned in 1864 the duty of buying items for the Office of Provisions and Clothing.[6]

Bulloch was furnished with about $600,000 in drafts on London banks and in letters of credit. As soon as these sources of cash were exhausted, the Confederate States treasury began to improvise expedients such as bonds and treasury notes backed by nothing except the faith of the government. Cotton in the Confederacy was used to back notes which were sharply discounted because of the difficulty in running the blockade.

The expedient of shipping cotton out of the Confederacy to pay specific debts next became prevalent, with the bales of cotton bearing marking to indicate Navy Department general funds, Office of Ordnance and Hydrography, and so on. This system provided cash, but it lacked flexibility; one account might have a temporary money surplus while another had goods ready for shipment but lacked funds to pay for it. The situation got so bad that the President directed Secretary of State Benjamin to devise a solu-

---

5. *Ibid.*, 771, 790.
6. *Ibid.*, 675.

tion. The result was that all funds in Europe were turned over to Colin J. McRae who disbursed them in accordance with instructions from the various departments.[7] He was also to be furnished the large amounts contemplated from loans being negotiated for the Confederacy by the French firm of Emile Erlanger and Company. In the last months of the war, when it became evident that no more navy ships could be got to sea from Europe and those under construction were sold, navy funds held by McRae were transferred to the army accounts.

Bulloch bought and got to sea the *Florida*, *Alabama*, and *Shenandoah*. Matthew F. Maury acquired an antiquated and unsatisfactory ship which went to sea under his cousin, William L. Maury, as CSS *Georgia*. Maury also bought the *Rappahannock*, a former British government ship, but got her no further than Calais, where she was detained by the French government. These ships and the cruisers fitted out in the Confederacy sank more than two hundred Union merchant ships, fishing craft, and whaling vessels. These were impressive accomplishments but they may not have been worth their enormous cost in money, diplomatic effort, and professional officer personnel. It is generally conceded that the cruiser warfare had no appreciable effect upon the course of the war.

The ironclad program offered the greatest potential reward of all the Confederate naval effort. It was no great trick to contract for building ironclads in either England or France. Private builders in both countries were happy to undertake the construction once funds were available, and foreign navy departments were glad for builders to gain experience with new designs. However, United States diplomats were quite vigilant in detecting ironclad construction and aggressive in preventing delivery. Where

7. *Ibid.*, ser. 1, II, 196–198.

subterfuge was possible in sailing a cruiser, an ironclad was so distinctive and construction took so long that getting it out without government connivance was practically impossible.

The plan which Mallory proposed contemplated several ironclads making a simultaneous sortie, crossing the ocean at the same time and bursting on a surprised Union fleet at New Orleans, Wilmington, Charleston, or some other place. The probability of success for such an action, even without diplomatic interference, was so small as to be hardly worthy of consideration. New ships break down; storms come unexpectedly; seas treat different ships in different ways.

The *Stonewall* was the only Confederate ironclad to leave a European port. She sailed in early 1865, broke down several times off the coast of France and Spain, and reached the western Atlantic after Lee's surrender. She was turned over to the Captain General of Cuba, a successful vessel, but too late to participate in the war for which she was built. Had she arrived six months earlier, she might with luck have temporarily broken the blockade at Charleston, Savannah, or Wilmington. Even then, her draft was so great that she could only have entered port under very favorable circumstances, and would surely have been sunk by an overwhelming concentration of Union monitors. The cruise of the *Stonewall* was an exercise in futility.

Blockade runners fitted out in Europe had more success. Most of these vessels were commercial or state ventures in which the Confederate Navy's only interest was as a shipper. By the autumn of 1863, the Confederate army and navy were entitled to one third of the cargo space of any commercial blockade runner.[8]

A number of the blockade runners were government-

---

8. *Ibid.*, ser. 2, II, 564.

chartered. Generally these ships were manned by civilians but were often commanded by Confederate naval officers on leave. Bulloch or his army counterpart, Caleb Huse, negotiated the charter; and Bulloch or Barron assigned the captain from available naval officers.

A few blockade runners were owned by the Confederacy. Bulloch brought the *Fingal* over in 1861 with probably the most urgently needed cargo of the war, arms and ammunition for the Shiloh campaign. By 1864 a regular line of blockade runners was being run for the navy, with many of the ships making a direct voyage from Europe and others from Bermuda or the Bahamas. A proposal to construct armored vessels to run cotton out of the Confederacy was wisely scotched in 1862.

Josiah Gorgas, the army's chief of ordnance, proposed that the navy take control of blockade running, but the navy refused to consider blockade running its business until late in the war. In March 1864, Mallory established Lieutenant John Wilkinson in Wilmington, as recounted on page 66. No regular office in Bermuda or the Bahamas was ever set up by the navy for the management of blockade runners. This omission was a grave error because often government cargo of great importance waited a long time while luxury items paying high profits were promptly embarked.

In the early days of the war, Mallory himself ordered the material to be imported, usually through Bulloch. Quantities were modest, specifications general, and cost was carefully considered. Later, enormous quantities were ordered and cost seemed to be of little moment. Mallory's letters were never very precise as to exact quality, size, or composition. He was often so general that it was difficult to determine his wants. By 1864 the individual offices in the

Navy Department were making their own demands upon the European representatives, using appropriated funds or their cotton equivalents to pay.

The Office of Ordnance and Hydrography ordered heavy guns (up to thirteen inches) of various designs, including those of Armstrong, Whitworth, and Blakely. It ordered vast amounts of ammunition, and armor plate as well as tools, laboratory equipment, and small arms. Lieutenant Murdaugh had to find and buy technical publications for Brooke; Maury and Davidson bought miles of insulated wire, Wheatstone batteries, and similar equipment for their submarine mines.

The Office of Provisions and Clothing directed the purchase of buttons, insignia, and uniforms similar to those worn by the British Navy. The Marine Corps bought clothing through navy channels. The office of Medicine and Surgery contracted for drugs as well as instruments. The Secretary ordered stationery, printed forms, office supplies. The Secretary even directed Bulloch to hire artisans to work in navy industrial establishments.

Bulloch observed that it would be difficult to get warships to sea from Europe because enemy diplomats would be sure to insist upon English and French neutrality, and enemy warships would be patrolling European waters. His fears were well founded. As an alternative, in 1864 he proposed that plans be drawn up in the Confederacy for ships, including ironclads, and sent to him abroad. He would then buy and ship out components such as engines, boilers, armor plate, shafts, pumps, propellers, and guns. The items would be fitted in Europe and then broken up into the largest transportable pieces and marked for reassembly at the building sites. Rivets, tools, and complete directions would accompany the machinery. The hull and other wooden work which was bulky and relatively easy to fashion would be built in the Confederacy.[9] The idea was adopted, but inefficiency in Richmond prevented its being a complete success.

As stated earlier, poor financial arrangements made the work of the European representatives difficult. The decision to hold cotton off the market in 1860–1861 turned out to be disastrous from a military and naval point of view, whatever its diplomatic merits might have been. Bulloch had little money and North seldom had any. A good portion of their efforts was always expended in stalling creditors or borrowing money from friends.

Regardless of what was planned, Bulloch became financial agent for the entire naval organization abroad, at least until McRae took over the function of paying contractors and Barron assumed the role of commander-in-chief of the officers and men awaiting assignment to ships. Bulloch or his subordinate paid the officers and men and remitted allotments to dependents in Europe, all in gold. He advanced money to officers sent home by commercial transportation. He furnished cruising funds to the ships, usually in the form of letters of credit, though sometimes in sterling currency. After the *Sumter*, *Georgia*, and *Rappahannock* were decommissioned and the *Alabama* was sunk, he paid off their crews. When the ironclads which could not be delivered were sold, the money was turned over to McRae for general use abroad.

In addition to financial matters, a number of administrative responsibilities had to be fulfilled for the many Confederates in Europe. It was Mallory's initial plan to send officers abroad barely in time to embark in the newly

---

9. *O.R.N.*, ser. 2, II, 184.

built or purchased ships. This was found impracticable because the time of sailing was unpredictable and because officers became stranded when ships were sold or sunk.

Until Barron arrived, the task of managing officers devolved on Bulloch as senior officer in Europe. Barron took this responsibility upon himself, with Matthew F. Maury acting for him when he was absent. Thus Barron's became a sub-office of Orders and Detail. From time to time, particularly toward the end of the war, he reduced the number of idle officers by ordering them home. When it became assured in December 1864 that his own squadron of ironclads would not get out, he recommended his own return to the dying Confederacy.

Particularly important to the success of Bulloch and his associates was the procurement of men capable of thwarting Union spies and running vessels destined for Confederate service out of European ports. Bulloch had two men whom he considered reliable for this work, Eugene L. Tessier and John Low. He ultimately got Low a commission as lieutenant in the Confederate Navy although he was a British subject.

Almost all the sailors who manned Confederate ships abroad were foreigners, induced to enlist by high pay, bounty, prospective prize money, a sense of adventure, or a desire to be freed from jail. The majority were British, though the cruisers often recruited Union sailors from their prizes. There were a few Southerners, mostly men who had come out in the *Sumter* or *Florida* or who were otherwise stranded abroad. Going to sea had been a very unusual occupation for the antebellum Southerner. Until Barron took charge as commander-in-chief, Bulloch was responsible for the management of these men.

Available records indicate that the transactions of all

the naval officers in Europe were honestly conducted. Officers approached with offers of bribes or fee splitting reported to their comrades and to their superiors. Instances of fraud on the part of Confederate naval agents abroad would be hard to detect, but the absence of accusations against any of them is very much in their favor.

If one accepts the broad policies of the Confederate government, it is difficult to find fault with the organization and administration employed in Europe. The keystone of the policy was the assumption that a threatened or actual cotton famine would bring about financial, material, and possibly military assistance to the Confederacy by England or France or both. Had this assumption been sound, the flow of armored ships and other vital materials might have been adequate to make up for the industrial backwardness of the South. While this might not have brought victory to the outnumbered Confederates, it almost certainly would have prolonged the conflict, increased division and war weariness in the North, and made far more difficult the restoration of the Union.

Wise government needs to look beyond hopeful policy and into reality, and this is what the Confederate Navy Department failed to do. It sent North to Europe without funds and with instructions to buy ironclad war vessels expected to cost at least two million dollars and get them to sea. Bulloch told Mallory as early as November 1863 that the ironclads would not be delivered, but only in the last few months of the war would the Secretary agree to their sale.[10]

The cruiser policy was almost as hopeless. The British had twice suffered from American cruiser and privateer warfare. As the dominant shipping nation, it was England's correct policy to prevent the interference of irregular sea

---

10. *O.R.N.*, ser. 2, II, 523–527.

forces with her shipping. She had achieved a triumph in naval diplomacy in 1856 by getting most of the important nations of the world (except the United States) to outlaw war against commerce. The Confederacy proposed to tear down that legal wall. There were a few brief times when individual influence or subterfuge were able to circumvent Britain's traditional policy, but there was never any serious likelihood that the policy would be abandoned.[11]

The purchase of munitions and the running of the blockade were quite another thing. There seems to have been no question about the legitimacy of permitting a warring nation to buy goods, and neither British nor French governments seriously made any real effort to prevent their nationals from running the blockade. The Confederates might have saved themselves a great deal of money and also insured priority to essential cargoes had they from the beginning made blockade running a naval instead of a commercial operation.

Bulloch's idea of prefabrication should have been adopted and extended. British naval architects could have been given the basic requirements for ships including ironclads, and paid to draw up complete plans. Those parts which took special skills, the machines, and critical material could then have been built in British factories while duplicate plans for wooden hulls and similar bulky and easy-to-build items could have been sent to the Confederacy. Hull and machinery could have been built simultaneously. When the English-built parts were ready and marked, they could have been sent for installation in the hulls. This system was feasible; it had been successfully tried in Savannah, Georgia, as early as 1834.[12]

The results of the overseas purchasing commissions were good. The timely arrival of Bulloch's *Fingal* in No-

---

11. See also Frank L. Owsley, *King Cotton Diplomacy* (Chicago, 1931), 418–449.
12. Alexander R. Lawton, "An Address by Alexander R. Lawton," *Georgia Historical Quarterly* III (June 1919), 52.

vember 1861 with her load of gunpowder, firearms, and clothing alone made the remainder of the effort worthwhile. It is not possible to estimate the total value or volume of naval materials that arrived in the Confederacy, but they were enormous.

Naval inspectors, particularly in ordnance, rejected items bought in Europe which did not come up to specifications. Rapid delivery was not to be expected. Much time was required to establish full production rates; but, once material began coming out, orders were quickly filled. Losses or delays en route were sometimes excessive. When ships could sail directly from Europe to southern ports, delivery was prompt; but it became increasingly difficult to bring ocean-going ships through the blockade. The institution of a line of navy blockade runners out of Bermuda in 1864 was a late but sensible step toward a practical solution. A blockade running headquarters in these islands similar to the one established in Wilmington would have been a logical next step, but the time was too late for any great benefit to be realized from organized blockade running under naval control.

21

Operational Command[1]

THE Secretary of the Navy had military command of the navy, subject to the President's authority as commander in chief. Orders of an important military nature usually bore the Secretary's signature and those which did not included the phrase "By command of the Secretary of the Navy." In either case it was the responsibility of the Office of Orders and Detail to prepare the orders.

The Secretary used a simple dictionary code for secret communications which might fall into the hands of the enemy. It is described in a 16 June 1861 letter from Semmes to Mallory:

> I have the honor to enclose herewith a copy of "Reid's English Dictionary," a duplicate of which I retain, for the purpose mentioned in your letter of instructions, of the 7th instant. I have not been able to find in the city of New Orleans, "Cobb's Miniature Lexicon," suggested by you, or any other suitable dictionary, with but a single column on a page. This need make no difference, however. In my communications to the Department, should I have occasion to refer to a word in the copy sent, I will designate the first column on the page, A, and the second column, B. Thus, if I wish to use the word "prisoner," my reference to it would be as follows: 323, B, 15; the first number referring to the page, the letter to the column, and the second number to the number of the word from the top of the column.[2]

---

1. A list of operational commanders is given in the Appendix.
2. *O.R.N.*, ser. 1, I, 615–616.

Until 1863, the chain of operational command led from the Secretary to the commander of an area command; for instance, the commander of naval forces for the defense of Georgia and South Carolina. This officer either commanded his war vessels in person or through a subordinate commander appointed by him for a particular operation. The latter was generally the highest ranking officer of the ships participating, but was sometimes an officer with no other assignment.

After March 1863, the commander of the station was no longer in the chain of command for operations. The Secretary ordered officers to permanent duty commanding naval forces afloat and designated the ships comprising the command. The commander of naval forces afloat was sometimes called the squadron commander; and his unit, a squadron. He normally held the temporary rank of flag officer while in this assignment.

A flag officer afloat had a staff whose size varied with the importance of the command, the desires of the commander, and the availability of officers and men. The captain of the flagship, designated staff or flag captain, acted as chief of staff and deputy commander. A lieutenant, almost always an ordnance expert, was flag lieutenant and ordnance officer. It was his duty to prepare orders to subordinates and to recommend the targets for each ship. Two or more midshipmen or master's mates acted as aides, delivering the flag officer's orders to the captain of the flagship or, by boat, signal flag, or signal light to the other ships. These aides sometimes were sent ashore to observe enemy ship movements, reporting by messenger. The flag officer's secretary recorded the minutes of the action if he were present, although the secretary was often left behind to maintain liaison with army or navy units ashore. Sometimes one or more army signal officers were also embarked to facilitate interservice or intership communications. In battle, the flag officer's surgeon worked as a member of the flagship's medical aid force, and the engineer advised the commander on engineering problems. The enlisted members of the staff consisted of the boat coxswain, steward, and cook.

Flag officers issued letters of instructions to their subordinates, including commanders of naval shore batteries. The instructions gave brief descriptions of the commander's intended action under various circumstances, but did not usually require action until a signal was executed. Flag officers discussed letters of instruction with subordinate commanders, if possible, and solicited their opinions before officially transmitting the letters to the ships. Flag officers also issued standing orders for matters of a more permanent or routine nature. Neither letters of instruction nor standing orders were standardized as to form or content.

A signal book was provided to each vessel and unit commander to facilitate tactical communications. Daytime signals were transmitted by varicolored flags, different combinations of which had meanings set down in the signal book. For night signalling, colored lights were hoisted above, below, or alongside each other to give appropriate messages. Whistle signals and pyrotechnics were also used.[3]

The command organization, patterned on that long in use in the United States Navy, was familiar and simple. The higher ship speeds and restricted maneuvering areas made necessary improved means of communication over those used before the war. As in any military setup, the character and intelligence of the commanders and the arms available to them had far greater bearing on combat performances than the organization and communications they employed.

---

3. *O.R.N.*, ser. 1, XXIII, 123.

Hence, failures on the part of the Confederate Navy's operational commanders should be attributed primarily to commanders and equipment and not the organization.

After the command of forces afloat was separated from that of the station, a new set of command relations had to be established, since neither of the two commanders had authority over the other. The situation was potentially troublesome because the station commandant was responsible for furnishing stores, personnel, and repairs to the flag officer afloat, usually much his junior in age, experience, and permanent rank. Surprisingly, there was almost no conflict, a tribute to the tact and patriotism of both groups.

The commandant of a station had a staff which included a lieutenant for ordnance officer and aide, a surgeon, a paymaster, and an engineer. The naval activities ashore in the area, such as ordnance works, receiving ships, storekeeper, hospitals, and marine detachments were under his military command. Many of the activities also had responsibilities to officers in charge or other seniors in Richmond who issued orders directly to them, usually without informing the commandant of the station. The commandant was expected to keep himself and the Navy Department informed on matters of naval construction; and, in case of emergency, he sometimes took a partially completed ship away from builders in order to complete or destroy her.

The flag officer afloat had responsibility for the naval shore batteries in his vicinity as well as for the ships assigned to his squadron. He issued instructions for their government, shifted men back and forth between ships and batteries, and coordinated the two forces in attack or defense. Naval batteries were organized after the manner of ships, operated their guns in seagoing fashion, and used nautical nomenclature. The commanders of naval batteries were not allowed to order summary courts-martial, that authority being reserved to commanders afloat.

Naval batteries afforded one of several types of contact between navy and army. The character of interservice command relationships varied with the personal characteristics of the commanders and with other circumstances.

The simplest relationship involved a naval officer detailed to army service either in his naval rank or in a temporary army rank. He had the same authority and prerogatives as any army officer serving in the position, and he made no reports to the navy. Early in the war, there were some difficulties when naval officers had to be assigned to instruct army batteries commanded by officers senior to them.

The assignment of a naval vessel or other unit to an army command was more complicated. This happened often in the early part of the war and was standard practice in the trans-Mississippi area throughout the conflict. The naval commander acted as a subordinate unit commander in the army, and moved his ship in accordance with orders. This was the situation of Lieutenant Isaac Brown, whose ship, the *Arkansas*, was assigned to General Earl Van Dorn's command. Oddly, William F. Lynch, the flag officer over Brown, remained independent of Van Dorn. The ship performed her assigned duties brilliantly. She was later lost on an army mission to Baton Rouge for which she was not properly prepared and on which she should not have been sent.[4]

The assignment of naval vessels to army command almost always reflected the desire of the local army officer and almost never that of the naval officer involved. Navy officers believed that they were the best judges of their own forces' capabilities and limitations. Army officers, con-

---

4. *Ibid.*, XIX, 130.

sidering that they were responsible for the protection of areas in which naval vessels represented a large portion of defensive strength, felt that they should have authority to issue detailed instructions to individual vessels without having to obtain the concurrence of flag officers to whose command the ships were assigned.

Logic appears on the side of the army, insofar as river and harbor warfare is concerned. Movement is so restricted that usual naval freedom of action is lost; movement becomes linear. Position is often more important than material victory. It was a hard thing for naval officers with many years of experience in high command to subordinate themselves to young army commanders ashore, but this practice should have become the rule on most of the Confederacy's inland waters.

An opposite command relation might have been devised for such places as Charleston, Mobile, and New Orleans, where there was so much water that it governed military as well as naval operations. In North Carolina waters, this system was used early in the war and deserved better results than could be achieved with the small force available. Late in the war there were disputes between General William H. C. Whiting and Flag Officer William F. Lynch in the Wilmington area, where the navy had had primary interest and should have had overall command.[5]

The failure of army and navy commanders to work smoothly together was too widespread to be attributed solely to personality conflicts or even to service pride. There were deep philosophical differences between the two groups. Friction between army and navy leaders was not peculiar to the Confederacy or to the Civil War but is as old as the services themselves.

5. *Ibid.*, VIII, 8, 865–867; *O.R.A..* ser. 1, LI, pt. 2, 829–830, 833.

22

Shipboard Routine

THE guide for shipboard organization was *Ordnance Instructions*, either the United States Navy original or its Confederate adaptation.[1] The manual gave detailed sample organizations for several classes of sailing or steam ships, but it was not intended to be used without modification for the peculiarities of a particular ship. Sails played an important part in the instructions, since all prewar vessels relied upon sail for propulsion, at least in part.

In all emergencies, the captain was stationed on the quarterdeck in the vicinity of the wheel or compass, in general charge of the ship. The executive officer (sometimes called the first lieutenant by old-fashioned officers) was with the captain and was expected to take active charge of working the ship; that is, managing the sails. The master was also stationed on the quarterdeck to assist on matters of seamanship and navigation. The captain's clerk made notes for a narrative of the action. Two or more midshipmen aides to the commanding officer delivered his orders to stations out of hearing of the quarterdeck and performed duty as signal officers. Most of the men in that area belonged to the master's division: quartermaster for helmsman, signalmen, men to take soundings, topmen for the mastheads,

---

1. U. S. Navy Department, *Instructions in relation to the preparation of vessels of war for battle: to the duties of officers and others when at quarters: and to ordnance and ordnance stores* (Washington, 1852); Confederate States Navy Department, *Ordnance Instructions for the Confederate States Navy relating to the preparation of vessels of war for Battle to the duties of officers and others when at quarters to Ordnance and Ordnance Stores and to Gunnery.* Third Edition (London, 1864).

and the like. The boatswain, who was a subordinate of the master, took station on the forecastle, ready to let go the anchor, to lower a boat, or to supervise any other evolution of seamanship.

The gun divisions were in the charge of lieutenants with midshipmen assistants. Each lieutenant of a gun division was responsible for casting loose and preparing his guns for action. The number of guns assigned a division depended upon the size of the crew required and the arrangement of guns on the ship. Allowances of personnel contemplated manning guns on only one broadside at a time, with a capability to man both sides simultaneously at a reduced rate of fire for a short time. Pivot guns were allowed complete crews. A gun division might be assigned only one very heavy pivot gun or as many as six smaller guns, three on each side. Gun crews varied in number from as few as eleven on a 32-pounder smooth bore to twenty-seven for a large caliber pivot rifle. A gun crew was in charge of its first gun captain, usually a boatswain's mate. A gunner's mate or quarter gunner from the powder division was assigned to each gun division in action.

In addition to manning the heavy guns, gun divisions were required to detail trimmers on call to make minor changes in sail. They were also organized into boarding parties which consisted of all the petty officers and most of the best seamen, and which were to be ready when ordered. Less experienced men from the gun crew were detailed as pikemen to repel enemy boarders. The gun crew also furnished some fire fighters, equipped with buckets.

The marine detachment usually manned smaller guns under their own officer but sometimes augmented sailor crews. When ordered, they acted as sharpshooters or formed part of boarding or pike parties.

The other division concerned with gunnery was the powder division, commanded by a lieutenant and including the gunner and his mates. The lieutenant remained on deck, whence he sent orders prescribing projectiles and propulsion charges to the gunner in the principal magazine and his senior assistants in lesser magazines and shell rooms. Before battle, men of the powder division rigged wet canvas screens about magazine openings, donned special smock-like dress and canvas shoes, and divested themselves of all metal objects. Their work was made dangerous by the presence of numbers of immature powder boys whose duty it was to carry the powder from magazine opening to the guns. The gunner and his mates had to be ready instantly to flood ammunition spaces in case of fire.

The chief engineer remained in the engine room, but his officers and men continued to operate on watches, four to six each engine and each boiler. The off-duty men were organized into fire-fighting and repair parties, with excess men available to augment gun crews when directed.

The surgeon and his assistants took station in the wardroom with instruments, bandages, and drugs available for the wounded, who were to come to them or be brought by members of their gun crew or working spaces. The paymaster was in his office, available to open storerooms for repair of damage, while his clerk guarded the spirit room from fire or looting. The carpenter was supplied with wooden shot plugs, timber for shoring, and apparatus for sounding tanks. It was his duty to report leakage, but only to the captain or executive officer, and then in a low voice. The sailmaker rigged handpumps, hoses, and prepared to repair damaged canvas.

The individual sailor's duties were assigned on a watch, quarter, and station bill signed by the commanding officer and posted in a conspicuous place on the ship. This schedule listed the important evolutions through which a ship's crew could expect to be put. With the battle organization as the starting point, men were assigned by name to boarding, pikeman, fire and maneuvering stations, as well as to specific responsibilities for the maintenance of equipment and cleaning.

The ship's crew was divided into two equal groups, the port and starboard watches, either of which was supposed to be able to get the ship underway and operate for a short time. The watches were divided into two or three sections, each capable of keeping guard in port until the remainder of the crew could be called to duty. When liberty ashore was allowed only one section, one sixth to one fourth of the crew was normally to be allowed ashore.

The call to battle stations for muster was by drum beat. If men were to cast loose the guns and break out such battle equipment as guns, rammers, sponges, and shoring, the beat was to be followed by a single roll of the drum; and, if the call was for action and magazines were to be opened, two rolls followed the beat to quarters. A rattle, something like that used at New Year's parties, sounded the call for boarders. A gong called away pikemen. Rapid ringing of the bell by the ship's cook was the fire alarm. In each case the boatswain and his mates went from hatch to hatch repeating the orders verbally. The master at arms and ship's corporals routed out laggards and patrolled spaces below deck.

Conditions on the Confederate ironclads required a number of departures from the organization and procedures outlined in this manual. The most important of these changes resulted from the entire removal of gear associated with wind propulsion. Except for the captain and the pilot, who had to take exposed positions in order to control the vessel's movement, the crew was afforded protection of heavy armor. The manning requirements of the guns determined the size of the deck force rather than the necessity for sailors to work sails; hence all guns were supposed to be fully manned all the time when the ship was at battle stations. The new arrangements freed the executive officer from his duties in managing sails and made him available to take charge of the guns, often with the additional title of "Ordnance Officer." The lieutenants likewise became more gunnery-minded. Thus additional officers became available from the sails just as other circumstances demanded additional officers to help operate the guns.

There were several reasons why the proportion of officers assigned to guns had to be increased. Guns were larger and more complex than before the war. They were fired at shorter and longer ranges than before: shorter to penetrate heavy armor and longer because Union vessels were so much faster that they were able to evade close action when they desired.

When it became evident that shots from neither side could easily penetrate the other's armor, boarding parties took on a new importance after years of disuse, and boarding parties always used a high proportion of officers. Mallory's fertile mind encouraged plans for the use of boarders equipped with bars and wedges to jam turrets and with blankets and burning sulphur and explosives to blind and suffocate enemy crews. Ships conducted drills in these new techniques, but none is known to have used them in action.

The main reason for the increased ratio of officers to enlisted men in gunnery stations was a decrease in the number of both officers and men who were experienced in their duties. Casualties, desertions, illness, erratic transfer policies, and temporary detachments to form commando parties or to man shore batteries all cut into permanence of gun crews until quite frequently officers, men, and gun met for the first time en route to battle. Perhaps twenty per cent of the Confederate Navy was absent from primary duty at any one time and often entire ships were temporarily abandoned only to be fully manned again in a few weeks.

Another change that had to be made from the traditional organization to suit the new ironclads was a reduction in the time spent aboard ship. Ironclads were singularly uncomfortable and unhealthful. Their armor transmitted heat or cold from the atmosphere to the interior and retained it there. They were leaky and humid below decks. Gasses from the boiler furnaces often permeated the living spaces. By 1863 it was customary for the crew to eat and sleep in a tender, a receiving ship, or ashore in warehouses or tents, leaving the ship in care of a section of watch. Each morning, at mealtimes, and in the evenings, officers and men had to be ferried back and forth at sacrifice of time and readiness.

23

Conclusion

IT is remarkable that the Confederate Navy accomplished as much as it did under the handicaps it suffered. Ships were built from poor plans, of inferior materials, and manned by makeshift crews. In battle they were almost always outnumbered. The Confederate Navy was more an officers' navy than the army was an officers' army, a fact which probably accounts for the destruction of so many ships by their own forces; Confederate naval officers were able to judge when the odds for victory were hopeless. There is good reason to believe that the Confederate Navy would have served the nation better had it been less professional in its outlook and continued each fight until the last ship had been sunk and the last man fallen.

In a broad sense, it was psychological error and material inferiority which led to the ineffectiveness of the Confederate Navy; but organization and administration were also at fault. There were not enough sailors and junior officers and too many older officers. The pilot problem was poorly handled, as was that of engineer officers. Ship construction and design, especially draft and engineering, were badly mismanaged in Richmond.

The Marine corps fulfilled its mission, although it,

like the naval school, was a severe drain on the South's limited resources. The supply and medical sections of the navy did their jobs as well as circumstances permitted. Confederate naval ordnance was superb, far better than might have been expected.

The navy's shortcomings were due in large measure to lack of aggressive leadership on the part of the Secretary. It was he who should have insisted upon the navy's getting a fair share of men. He was the man to shelve deadwood at the top and to conserve manpower at the bottom, but it was he who encouraged and approved eccentric operations which drained off the best officers and men for spectacular but pointless expeditions. He was the appropriate official to secure an adequate supply of industrial workers.

Unfortunately for the Confederacy, Mallory was a dreamer and a romantic. He kept hoping things would somehow work themselves out if left alone. A lover of innovation and a progressive thinker, he failed to take sufficient cognizance of the means by which some of his ideas were to be applied. Ever proud of his cabinet position, he refused to risk it in an all-out effort to obtain the men, money, and material essential to the navy's well-being. He was likewise reluctant to risk the navy in battle, and his commanders knew it. It was his and their habit to conserve their ships until the enemy approached in overwhelming force ashore and afloat. Then Mallory's commanders destroyed their own vessels to keep them from falling into enemy hands. This happened without censure so often that one is almost forced to conclude that Confederate naval policy was averse to fighting. The role of the weaker naval power is never an easy one since the only logical course of action open is to retire from the scene of conflict and conduct a warfare of attrition. In the instance of the Confederacy, blockade at one end and shallow water at the other prevented withdrawal. Well-laid minefields might have afforded protection for occasional forays on unwary and unsupported enemy vessels, but they would have been worthwhile only if the Confederacy had been willing to risk her ships. Without such willingness, the Confederate Navy was itself doomed to attrition.

Appendix

Uniform and Dress of the
Navy of the Confederate States*

UNDRESS [Sea Officers] COAT

For a Flag Officer, shall be a frock coat of steel grey cloth faced with the same and lined with black silk serge, double breasted, with two rows of large navy buttons on the breast, nine in each row, placed four inches and a half apart from eye to eye at top, and two inches and a half at bottom. Rolling collar, skirts to be full, commencing at the top of the hip bone and descending four-fifths thence towards the knee, with one button behind on each hip and one near the bottom of each fold. The cuffs to be two inches and a half deep, with one strip of gold lace one-half inch wide below the seam, but joining it; three strips of lace of the same width on the sleeve above the cuffs, separated by a space of three-eighths of an inch from each other, the upper one with a loop three inches long, and a strip of lace half an inch wide, from the lower button to the end of the cuffs on the upper side of the opening, and four small sized buttons (navy buttons) in the opening.

For a Captain, the same as for a Flag Officer, except that there shall be but three strips of lace around the sleeve and cuff, including the looped strip.

For a Commander, the same in all respects as for a Captain, except that there shall be but two strips of lace around the sleeve and cuff, including the looped strip, and three small buttons in the opening.

---

* From C. S. War Department, comp., *Uniform and Dress Army and Navy of the Confederate States* (Richmond, 1861).

For a Lieutenant, the same in all respects as for a Commander, except that the cuffs shall have but one strip of gold lace, looped, around the upper edge.

For a Master, the same as for a Lieutenant, except that the cuffs shall have but one strip of lace one-fourth of an inch wide, without a loop, around the upper edge.

For a Passed Midshipman, the same as for a Master, excepting that the cuffs shall have, instead of lace, three medium sized navy buttons around the upper edge.

For a Midshipman, the same as for a Passed Midshipman, except that medium sized buttons shall be substituted for the large buttons.

UNDRESS [Civil Officers] COAT

For a Surgeon of over twelve years' standing, shall be a frock coat of steel grey cloth, faced with the same, double breasted, rolling collar, with two rows of large navy buttons on the breast, nine in each row, proportioned for body and skirts the same as for a captain, skirts lined with black silk serge, one button behind on each hip, and one near the bottom of each fold of the skirts. Cuffs the same as for a commander, except that a plain strip of lace shall be substituted for the loop.

For a Surgeon of less than twelve years' standing, the same, except that there shall be one strip of lace around the cuff and sleeve.

For a Passed Assistant Surgeon, the same as for a Surgeon of less than twelve years' standing, except that the lace on the cuff shall be one-quarter of an inch wide.

For an Assistant Surgeon, the same as for a Surgeon, except that instead of lace there shall be three medium sized buttons on the cuff.

For a Paymaster of over twelve years' standing, the same as prescribed for a Surgeon over twelve years.

For a Paymaster of less than twelve years' standing, the same as for a Surgeon of less than twelve years.

For a Chief Engineer of more than twelve years' standing, the same as for a Surgeon of more than twelve years.

For a First Assistant Engineer, the same as for a Chief Engineer, except that there shall be but one strip of lace on the cuff one-quarter of an inch wide.

For a Second and Third Assistant, the same as for a First Assistant Engineer, except that instead of lace the cuffs shall have three medium sized buttons around the upper edge.

For a Chaplain, the same as for a Surgeon, except that it shall be single breasted, with one row of nine large navy buttons on the breast. The cuffs plain with three small buttons in the opening.

For a Professor and Commodore's Secretary, the same as for a Chaplain, except that there shall be eight buttons on the breast.

For a Clerk, the same as for a Secretary, except that there shall be but six buttons on the breast.

VEST

For all officers, steel grey or white, single breasted, standing collar, with nine small buttons in front, and not to show below the coat.

PANTALOONS

For all officers, shall be of steel grey cloth or white drill, made loose to spread well over the foot and to be worn over boots or shoes.

SHOULDER STRAPS

For a Flag Officer, of sky-blue cloth, edged with black, four inches long and one inch and three-eighths wide, bordered with an embroidery of gold one-quarter of an inch in width, with four stars in line at equal distances, the two on the ends six-tenths of an inch in diameter, and the two intermediate six-eighths of an inch in diameter.

For a Captain, the same as for a Flag Officer, except that there shall be three stars at equal distances, each six-tenths of an inch in diameter.

For a Commander, the same as for a Captain, except that there shall be but two stars.

For a Lieutenant, the same as for a Commander, except that there shall be but one star, in the centre.

For a Master, the same as for a Lieutenant, except that there shall be no star.

For a Passed Midshipman, a strip of gold lace four inches long and half an inch wide.

For a Surgeon of more than twelve years' standing, the same as for a Master, except they shall be of black cloth, with two sprigs of olive, crossed, embroidered in gold in the centre.

For a Surgeon of less than twelve years' standing, the same, except that there shall be but one sprig of olive.

For a passed Assistant Surgeon, the same as for a Surgeon, except that instead of sprigs of olive, there shall be an olive leaf embroidered in gold on each end.

For an Assistant Surgeon, the same as for a Passed Assistant Surgeon, without the leaves.

For a Paymaster, of more than twelve years' standing, the same as for a Surgeon of more than twelve years, except that the straps shall be of dark green cloth.

For a Paymaster, of less than twelve years standing, the same as for a Surgeon of less than twelve years, except that the straps shall be of dark green cloth.

For an Assistant Paymaster, the same as for an Assistant Surgeon, except that the straps shall be of dark green cloth.

For a Chief Engineer of more than twelve years standing, the same as for a Master, except that there shall be two sprigs of live oak embroidered in gold in the centre, and the straps shall be of dark blue cloth.

For a Chief Engineer of less than twelve years' standing, the same, except that there shall be but one sprig of live oak.

Cap of steel gray cloth, to be not less than three inches and a half, nor more than four inches in height, and not more than ten nor less than nine inches and a half at top, with patent leather visor, to be worn by all officers in service dress.

For a Flag Officer, the device shall be a foul anchor in an open wreath of live oak leaves, with four stars above the anchor, embroidered in gold as per pattern, on the front of the cap above a band of gold lace one inch and three quarters wide.

For a Captain, the same as for a flag officer, except that there shall be but three stars above the anchor, and the gold band shall be one and one half inches wide.

For a Commander, the same as for Captain, except that there shall be but two stars.

For a Lieutenant, the same as for a Commander, except that there shall be but one star.

For a Master, the same as for a Lieutenant, except that there shall be no star.

For a Passed Midshipman, a foul anchor without the wreath.

For a Surgeon, of over twelve years standing, a wreath of olive leaves with three stars, four tenths of an inch in diameter, embroidered in gold as per pattern, on the front of the cap, above a band of gold lace one inch and a quarter wide.

For a Surgeon, of less than twelve years standing, the same, except that there shall be two stars.

For a Passed Assistant Surgeon, the same as for a Surgeon, except that there shall be but one star.

For an Assistant Surgeon, the same as for a Surgeon, except that there shall be no star.

For a Paymaster, of over twelve years' standing, the same as for a Surgeon of over twelve years standing.

For a Paymaster, of less than twelve years, the same as for a Surgeon of less than twelve years.

For an Assistant Paymaster, the same as for an Assistant Surgeon.

For a Chief Engineer, of more than twelve years' standing, the same as for a Surgeon of more than twelve years, except that the leter E in the old English character shall be embroidered in gold below the stars.

For a Chief Engineer, of less than twelve years, the same, except that there shall be but two stars.

For Second and Third Assistant Engineers, the same as for a First Assistant Engineer, except that there shall be no stars.

BUTTONS

Buttons shall be of three sizes: large, medium, and small, and all of the same device, as per pattern.

SUMMER FROCK COAT

In summer or in tropical climates, officers may wear frock coats and pantaloons of steel grey summer cloth of the style and pattern herein prescribed, with medium size navy buttons.

JACKETS

May be worn as service dress by all officers when at sea, except when at general muster. To be of steel gray cloth or white drill linen with the same, double breasted, rolling collar, same number of small sized buttons on breast as for undress coat, open fly sleeve with four small buttons in the opening, with shoulder straps for appropriate grades.

STRAW HATS

In summer or in tropical climates, officers may also wear, except at general muster, white straw hats. The body of the hat to be six inches in height, and the rim three and a half inches in width.

OVER COATS

For all officers, shall be of steel gray cloth, double breasted, rolling collar, skirts to descend three inches below the knee, the same number of navy buttons, and similarly arranged as for undress coat. No buttons to be worn on the cuffs or pocket flaps. Officers entitled to shoulder straps will wear the same on their overcoats as directed for undress coats. Gray cloth cloaks may be worn in boats.

DRESS FOR PETTY OFFICERS AND CREW

Boatswain's Mates, Gunner's Mates, Carpenter's Mates, Sailmaker's Mates, Ship's Steward and Ship's Cook, will wear embroidered in black silk on the right sleeve of their grey jackets above the elbow in front, a foul anchor of not more than three inches length. The same device embroidered blue to be worn on the sleeves of their white frocks in summer.

All other petty officers except officers' stewards and yeomen will wear the same device on their left sleeves.

The outside clothing for petty officers, firemen, and coalheavers, seamen, ordinary seamen, landsmen and boys for muster, shall consist of gray cloth jackets and trousers, or gray woolen frocks with white duck cuffs and collars, black hats, black silk neckerchiefs and shoes, or boots in cold weather. In warm weather it shall consist of white frocks and trousers, black or white hats, as the commander may for the occasion direct, having proper regard for the comfort of the crew; black silk neckerchiefs and shoes. The collars and cuffs to be lined with blue cotton cloth, and stitched round with thread. Thick gray caps without visors may be worn by the crew at sea, except on holidays or at muster.

For a Boatswain, Gunner, Carpenter and Sailmaker, shall be of steel gray cloth, lined with the same; rolling collar, double breasted, two rows of large navy buttons on the breast, eight in each row; pointed pocket flaps, with three large buttons underneath each, showing one-half their diameter; three medium size buttons around each cuff, and two small ones in each opening; one button behind on each hip; one in the middle of each fold, and one in each fold near the bottom of the skirt. On each side of the collar to have one loop of three-quarters wide gold lace, to show one inch and a half wide, and four inches long, with a small size navy button in the point of each loop.

VI.—The following changes are ordered in the uniform:

Admirals will wear one stripe in addition to the number worn by Flag Officers on the sleeve, and one star additional in shoulder strap and cap ornament.

Lieutenants Commanding will wear one stripe in addition to the number worn by First Lieutenants on the sleeve.

First Lieutenants will wear the uniform prescribed for Lieutenants.

Second Lieutenants will wear the same uniform as First Lieutenants, except the star in the shoulder strap.

Lieutenants for the war the same as Second Lieutenants.

Naval Constructors will wear the same uniform as Chief Engineers, substituting buff in the ground of the shoulder strap for dark blue, and the letter "C" in the cap ornament for the letter "E."

First Assistant Engineer will wear the same uniform as Passed Assistant Surgeons, except that the ground of the shoulder strap shall be dark blue.

Second Assistant Engineers will wear the same uniform as Assistant Surgeons, except that the ground of the shoulder strap will be dark blue.

S. R. MALLORY,
*Sec'y of the Navy.**

---

* From *C. S. Navy Register 1863*, 2.

Issuing Prices of Navy Clothing, and Quantities to be issued under Act of Congress, approved 30th April, 1863†

In the three years.	Per annum.	ARTICLES OF ISSUE.	Estimated value.	Issuing price with 10 p. c. added.
1		Pea Jackets, ...	$13 70	$15 07
	1	Round Jackets, ...	9 45	10 40
		Flannel Jumpers, ...	1 92	2 12
	2	Cloth Trowsers, ...	5 40	5 94
		Satinet Trowsers, ...	3 45	3 80
	3	Canvas Duck Trowsers, . . .	1 65	1 82
	3	Barnsley Sheeting Frocks, . . .	1 68	1 85
	3	Flannel Overshirts, ...	2 75	3 03
	3	Flannel Undershirts, ...	1 62	1 79
	2	Flannel Drawers, ...	1 56	1 72
	4	Shoes, pair, ...	2 63	2 90
	4	Socks, pair, ...	86	95
		Mattresses,*	6 90	7 59
	2	Caps, ...	1 37	1 51
	2	Silk Handkerchiefs, ...	1 50	1 65
2		Blankets, ...	2 82	3 11

* This article, as well as Flannel, Sheeting and Duck, cannot now be issued.

† From Office of Provisions and Clothing *Circular*, June 3, 1863.

Pay Table of
The Officers of the Navy*

Grades	Pay per annum.
Admiral	$6,000 00
Captains—	
When commanding squadrons	5,000 00
All others on duty at sea	4,200 00
On other duty	3,600 00
On leave or waiting orders	3,000 00
Commanders—	
On duty at sea first five years after date of commission	2,825 00
On duty at sea second five years after date of commission	3,150 00
On other duty first five years after date of commission	2,662 00
On other duty second five years after date of commission	2,825 00
All other commanders	2,250 00
*Lieutenants Commanding—*At sea	2,550 00
First Lieutenants—	
On duty at sea	1,500 00
After seven years' sea-service in the navy	1,700 00
After nine years' sea-service in the navy	1,900 00
After eleven years' sea-service in the navy	2,100 00
After thirteen years' sea-service in the navy	2,250 00
On other duty	1,500 00
After seven years' sea-service in the navy	1,600 00
After nine years' sea-service in the navy	1,700 00
After eleven years' sea-service in the navy	1,800 00
After thirteen years' sea-service in the navy	1,875 00
On leave or waiting orders	1,200 00
After seven years' sea-service in the navy	1,266 00
After nine years' sea-service in the navy	1,333 00
After eleven years' sea-service in the navy	1,400 00
After thirteen years' sea-service in the navy	1,450 00
*Second Lieutenants—*Duty afloat	1,200 00
When on leave or other duty	1,000 00
Fleet Surgeons	3,300 00

* From *C. S. Navy Register 1863*, 26–29.

Grades	Pay per annum.
Surgeons—	
On duty at sea—	
For first five years after date of commission as surgeon	$2,200 00
For second five years after date of commission as surgeon	2,400 00
For third five years after date of commission as surgeon	2,600 00
For fourth five years after date of commission as surgeon	2,800 00
For twenty years and upwards after date of commission	3,000 00
On other duty—	
For first five years after date of commission as surgeon	2,000 00
For second five years after date of commission as surgeon	2,200 00
For third five years after date of commission as surgeon	2,400 00
For fourth five years after date of commission as surgeon	2,600 00
For twenty years and upwards after date of commission	2,800 00
On leave or waiting orders—	
For first five years after date of commission as surgeon	1,600 00
For second five years after date of commission as surgeon	1,800 00
For third five years after date of commission as surgeon	1,900 00
For fourth five years after date of commission as surgeon	2,100 00
For twenty years and upwards after date of commission	2,300 00
Passed Assistant Surgeons—	
On duty at sea	1,700 00
On other duty	1,500 00
On leave or waiting orders	1,000 00
Assistant Surgeons—	
On duty at sea	1,250 00
On other duty	1,050 00
On leave or waiting orders	800 00
Paymasters—	
On duty at sea—	
For first five years after date of commission	2,000 00
For second five years after date of commission	2,400 00
For third five years ater date of commission	2,600 00
For fourth five years after date of commission	2,900 00
For twenty years and upwards after date of commission	3,100 00
On other duty—	
For first five years after date of commission	1,800 00
For second five years after date of commission	2,100 00
For third five years after date of commission	2,400 00
For fourth five years after date of commission	2,600 00
For twenty years and upwards after date of commission	2,800 00

Grades	Pay per annum.
Paymasters—continued.	
On leave or waiting orders—	
For fourth five years after date of commission	$2,000 00
For second five years after date of commission	1,600 00
For third five years after date of commission	1,800 00
For fourth five years after date of commission	2,000 00
For twenty years and upwards after date of commission	2,250 00
Assistant Paymaster—Duty afloat	1,200 00
Other duty	1,100 00
Masters, (in the line of promotion.)	
On duty as such at sea	1,000 00
On leave or other duty	900 00
Masters, (not in line of promotion.)	
On duty as such at sea	1,000 00
On leave or other duty	900 00
Passed Midshipmen—	
On duty as such at sea	900 00
When on leave or other duty	800 00
Midshipmen—	
At sea	550 00
On other duty	500 00
On leave or waiting orders	450 00
Boatswains, Gunners, Carpenters, and Sailmakers—	
On duty at sea—	
For first three years' sea-service from date of warrant	1,000 00
For second three years' sea-service from date of warrant	1,150 00
For third three years' sea-service from date of warrant	1,250 00
For fourth three years' sea-service from date of warrant	1,350 00
For twelve years' sea-service and upward	1,450 00
On other duty—	
For first three years' sea-service after date of warrant	800 00
For second three years' sea-service after date of warrant	900 00
For third three years' sea-service after date of warrant	1,000 00
For fourth three years' sea-service after date of warrant	1,100 00
For twelve years' sea-service and upwards	1,200 00
On leave or waiting orders—	
For first three years' sea-service after date of warrant	600 00
For second three years' sea-service after date of warrant	700 00
For third three years' sea-service after date of warrant	800 00
For fourth three years' sea-service after date of warrant	900 00

Grades	Pay per annum.
Boatswains, Gunners, Carpenters, and Sailmakers—On leave—continued.	
For twelve years' sea-service and upwards	1,000 00
Engineers	
Chief Engineers—On duty—	
For first five years after date of commission	1,800 00
For second five years after date of commission	2,200 00
For third five years after date of commission	2,450 00
After fifteen years from date of commission	2,600 00
On leave or waiting orders—	
For first five years after date of commission	1,200 00
For second five years after date of commission	1,300 00
For third five years after date of commission	1,400 00
After fifteen years from date of commission	1,500 00
First Assistant Engineers—	
On duty	1,250 00
On leave or waiting orders	900 00
Second Assistant Engineers—	
On duty	1,000 00
On leave or waiting orders	750 00
Third Assistant Engineers—	
On duty	750 00
On leave or waiting orders	600 00
Naval Storekeepers	1,700 00
Engineer-In-Chief	300 00
Naval Constructors	2,600 00
Naval Constructors, when not on duty	1,800 00
Secretaries to commanders of squadrons,	
when commanding-in-chief	1,000 00
Not commanding-in-chief	900 00
Navy Agents—	
	Pay pr m'th
Yeomen—	
In ships-of-the-line	49 00
In frigates	44 00
In sloops	34 00
In smaller vessels	28 00
Armorers—	
In ships-of-the-line	34 00
In frigates	29 00
In sloops	24 00

Grades	Pay per month
Mates—	
Master's, (not warranted)	29 00
Boatswain's	29 00
Gunners	29 00
Carpenter's	29 00
Sailmaker's	24 00
Armorer's	24 00
Master-at-Arms	29 00
Ship's Corporals	24 00
Coxswains	28 00
Quartermasters	28 00
Quarter Gunners	24 00
Captains—	
Of forecastle	28 00
Of tops	24 00
Of afterguard	24 00
Of hold	24 00
Coopers	24 00
Painters	24 00
Stewards—	
Ship's	34 00
Officer's	24 00
Surgeon's	28 00
Cooks—	
Ship's	28 00
Officer's	24 00
Masters of the Band	24 00
Musicians—	
First class	19 00
Second class	16 00
Seamen	22 00
Ordinary Seamen	18 00
Landsmen	16 00
Boys	12, 13 & 14
Firemen—	
First class	34 00
Second Class	29 00
Coal-Heavers	22 00

Naval Operational Commanders[1]

Virginia Area

Captain French Forrest [as Comdt of Norfolk Navy Yard, also commanded forces afloat]	10 July 1861–27 February 1862
Captain Franklin Buchanan	27 February–22 March 1862*
Captain Josiah Tattnall	29 March 1862–15 May 1862
Captain S. Smith Lee	15 May 1862–3 November 1862
Captain Samuel Barron	3 November 1862–24 March 1863*
Captain French Forrest	24 March 1863*–6 May 1864
Captain John K. Mitchell	7 May 1864–18 February 1865
Rear Admiral Raphael Semmes	18 February 1865–end of war

North Carolina Area

Commander, Naval Defense of the State of North Carolina

Captain Samuel Barron	to 29 August 1861
Captain William F. Lynch	3 September 1861–? July 1862
Unknown	July–November 1862
Captain William F. Lynch	? November 1862–13 Sept. 1864*
Captain Robert F. Pinkney	13 September 1864–end of war

Commander, Naval Forces Afloat, Inland Waters of North Carolina

Captain Robert F. Pinkney	? April 1864–13 September 1864
Captain James W. Cooke	13 September 1864–end of war

Georgia Area

Commander, Naval Defense of the State of Georgia

Captain Josiah Tattnall[2]	18 July 1861–22 March 1862
Lieutenant John Rutledge [as Senior officer Afloat]	22 March 1862–19 May 1862
Captain Josiah Tattnall	19 May 1862–31 March 1863

Commander, Naval Forces Afloat, Savannah

Commander Richard L. Page	31 March 1863–13 May 1863
Commander William A. Webb	13 May 1863–17 June 1863
Captain William W. Hunter	28 June 1863–end of war

---

1. This list is incomplete. The titles used are the ones most frequently employed in official correspondence; however the same officer was sometimes addressed in two or more different ways even by the Secretary of the Navy or the Officer in Charge of Orders and Detail.
* Throughout this appendix indicates approximate or presumed date.
2. Until 19 May 1862 the senior commander was in charge of naval defenses of both Georgia and South Carolina. This was Tattnall until 22

South Carolina Area

Commander, Naval Defense of the State of South Carolina

Captain Duncan F. Ingraham[2]   16 November 1861–7 April 1863

Commander, Naval Forces Afloat, Charleston

Captain John R. Tucker   7 April 1863—end of war

Commander, Naval Forces on the Pee Dee River

Alabama Area

Commander, Naval Forces in Defense of Mobile

Captain Victor M. Randolph	early 1861–20 September 1862
Admiral Franklin Buchanan	20 September 1862–5 August 1864
Captain Ebenezer Farrand	5 August 1864–end of war

Mississippi River Area

Commander, Naval Forces in Defense of the Coasts of Louisiana and the Mississippi

Captain Lawrence L. Rousseau	10 May 1861–1 August 1861
Captain George N. Hollins	1 August 1861–18 April 1862
Commander Robert F. Pinkney	18 April 1862–27 June 1862*
Captain William F. Lynch	27 June 1862*–10 October 1862*

Commander, Naval Forces Operating in the Vicinity of Fort Jackson and Fort Phillip

Commander John K. Mitchell   20 April 1862–29 April 1862

Trans-Mississippi Area

Commander, Naval Forces in Defense of Texas

Commander William W. Hunter	14 August 1861–22 April 1863
Lieutenant Joseph N. Barney	22 April 1863–?

Commander, Naval Forces, Trans-Mississippi Department

Commander Thomas W. Brent	[Prior] June 1863–September 1863*
Lieutenant Jonathan H. Carter	September 1863*–end of war

March 1862, when Ingraham succeeded him. When Tattnall returned to Savannah on 19 May 1862 he was made responsible for Georgia only.

Bibliographical Note

Manuscripts and Unpublished Theses

The most complete run of official correspondence used in this study was that of Captain William W. Hunter, C. S. Navy. Part of this material (Savannah Squadron Papers) is in the Emory Special Collections and part is in the Howard-Tilton Library at Tulane. Since Hunter was in positions of authority in Texas and Georgia throughout the war, the correspondence gives a fairly complete picture of administration on an intermediate level. The Howard-Tilton Library also has the correspondence of Captain Alfred C. Van Benthuysen, C. S. Marine Corps. Van Benthuysen was involved in so many disciplinary troubles that his papers are an excellent source for information on courts-martial.

Most of the important manuscript material in the National Archives that pertains to this study has been published by the Navy or War Departments. Record Group 45, Subject File VN, Navy Department Policies (Confederate Navy 1861–65), and Subject File VA, Administration and Organization of the Navy Department (internal), were searched without uncovering significant new material.

A typescript diary of Stephen R. Mallory (original in the Southern Historical Collection at the University of North Carolina) was read at the Library of Congress. At first glance this appears an invaluable source; it is perceptive, well written, and frank. It is also unfortunately typical of Mallory in promising much and failing in accomplishment. The diary starts on 30 May 1861 and stops on 18 September 1861. Then, omitting the critical period of the *Merrimack*, battle of New Orleans, and so on, it resumes on 15 May 1862 and continues to September 1862 where it stops until the war is over.

W. H. Purcell, "The Internal Administration of the Confederate States Navy" (Duke University, unpublished MA Thesis, 1937) was based almost entirely upon the reports of the Secretary of the Navy as reproduced in the official records. It is an incomplete but balanced treatment.

Confederate States Government Publications

Confederate Navy documents were largely revisions of those in use in the United States Navy at the time of secession.

Regulations of the Navy of the Confederate States (Richmond, 1862) provided the legal foundation for administration and gives much information on the duties of officers and men.

Register of the Commissioned and Warrant Officers of the Navy of the Confederate States, to January 1, 1863 (Richmond, 1862) and *Register of the Commissioned and Warrant Officers of the Navy of the Confederate States, to January 1, 1864* (Richmond, 1864) consist of published extracts from the register maintained by the Office of Orders and Detail. The *Register* was supposed to be an annual publication. It listed all the officers in order of rank, with information on sea or shore duty in both United States and Confederate Navies, and current duty assignment of each. An appendix included most of the laws pertaining to the navy, the administrative orders by the Secretary and the officer in charge of orders and detail, and latest changes in navy or uniform regulations. A shorter edition of *Register of the Commissioned and Warrant Officers of the Confederate States, to January 1, 1863* (n.p., but probably Richmond, 1863) includes only the data on officers.

Ordnance Instructions for the Confederate States Navy relating to the preparation of vessels of war for Battle to the duties of officers and others when at quarters to Ordnance and Ordnance Stores and to Gunnery, Third Edition (London, 1864) is a manual treating not only of ordnance subjects, but also giving much information concerning preparation for battle. Before the issuance of this book in 1864, Confederates had to rely on ordnance manuals prepared for the United States Navy. *Instructions for the Guidance of Medical Officers of the Navy* (Richmond, 1864) was the publication upon which much of Chapter 16 was based.

Examination papers [of midshipmen, prepared aboard the

Confederate States Schoolship *Patrick Henry*] (Richmond, 186–?) give information on examination subjects.

A Digest of the Military and Naval laws of the Confederate States from the Commencement of the Provisional Congress to the End of the First Congress under the Permanent Constitution (Columbia, 1864) is a convenient compilation of laws, some of which pertain to this study.

Uniform and Dress Army and Navy of the Confederate States (Richmond, 1861) was reproduced in facsimile by Raymond Riling and Roy Halter (New Hope, Pennsylvania, 1952). It includes illustrative plates as well as the regulations reproduced in Appendix I of this study. Changes in the regulations appear in the *Navy Registers*.

The Congressional investigation of the Confederate Navy Department initiated in September 1862 was haphazard, lengthy, and inconclusive, but much useful information was gleaned from the testimony, enclosures, and findings. A complete record is contained in *Report of Evidence taken before a Joint Special Committee of both Houses of the Confederate Congress to investigate the affairs of the Navy Department* (Richmond, 1863?). The report, less copies of shipbuilding contracts, is reprinted in *O.R.N.*, series 2, I, 431–809. The findings are in *Report from the Joint Select Committee to Investigate the Management of the Navy Department* (n.p., but apparently Richmond, 1863).

Proceedings of a Naval General Court Martial in the case of Captain Josiah Tattnall (Richmond, 1862) deals at length with the problems of pilots and with the lack of strategic direction by the Secretary of the Navy.

A number of single sheet or pamphlet copies of general orders or circulars issued by the Navy Department and not reprinted in the Navy Register were found in the Emory University Special Collections, the Howard-Tilton Library at Tulane University, and in the National Archives. It is believed that all the items in Marjorie Crandall, *Confederate Imprints* (2 vols., Boston, 1955) and Richard Harwell, *More Confederate Imprints* (2 vols., Richmond, 1957) applicable to this study have been seen.

United States Government Publications

The most useful and readily accessible source for a study of either navy in the Civil War are *The Official Records of the Union and Confederate Navies in the War of the Rebellion* (31 vols.; Washington, 1894–1927). The periodic reports of the Secretary of the Navy reprinted in *O.R.N.* were compared with the original printed documents when practicable. Discrepancies were minor with the exception of those of 30 April and 5 November 1864. *O.R.N.*, series 2, II, 631–639 (purportedly the report of 30 April 1864) are quoted from the report of 5 November 1864, pages 1–9, while *O.R.N.*, series 2, II, 743 to 749, printed as a portion of the report of 5 November 1864, actually belong in the April report. Fleet organizations for Savannah and Mobile shown on pages 630–631 and 743–744 also have their dates reversed.

Unfortunately missing from *O.R.N.* are Reports of the Secretary of the Navy dated 18 November 1861 and 10 January 1863, both mentioned in other correspondence but withheld from publication during the Civil War on account of secrets they contained. Search in major depositories failed to turn up a copy of either of the missing reports, though an uninformative hand-written fragment of the first was located in the National Archives (Record Group 45, Subject file VN, Box 680). Another printed fragment of the same report is in *O.R.N.*, series 2, I, 746. A spurious report, reproduced in *O.R.N.*, series 2, II, 598, was published by the United States for propaganda purposes on 31 December 1863.

United States War Department, comp., *The War of the Rebellion: A Compilation of the Official Records of the Union and Confederate Armies* (128 vols.; Washington, 1880–1901) is the companion set. It was valuable for interservice correspondence, especially about conscription, detail of artisans, and matters concerning prisoners of war.

Printed Diaries, Reminiscences, and Letters

This group of publications was disappointing. Participants usually either wrote long defenses of the right of secession and the tremendous sacrifices they made for a cause in which they did not particularly believe or wrote operational histories in which the first person singular figures prominently. Raphael Semmes, *Memoirs of Service Afloat* (New York, 1903) is an offender on both counts, but the book is absorbingly interesting and contains some helpful information on naval organization. Semmes administered his ships virtually independently of the Navy Department. More useful were William H. Parker, *Recollections of a Naval Officer, 1841–65* (New York, 1883), an excellent source for the navy school; John Wilkinson, *The Narrative of a Blockade Runner* (New York, 1877); and James D. Bulloch, *The Secret Service of the Confederacy in Europe* (2 vols.; London, 1883). John M. Kell, *Recollections of a Naval Life* (Washington, 1900) is mostly about operations in cruisers under Semmes but includes interesting letters concerning life aboard the James River ironclads in the last months of the war. James M. Morgan, *Recollections of a Rebel Reefer* (New York, 1917) is a first-rate adventure story which includes illuminating material on the navy as seen through the eyes of a ubiquitous and alert midshipman. Jefferson Davis, *Rise and Fall of the Confederate Government* (2 vols.; New York, 1881) contains little material about the navy.

Diaries by individuals outside the Confederate Navy furnished some interesting material on personalities. The best Confederate diary is Ben Ames Williams, ed., *A Diary from Dixie* by Mary Boykin Chesnut (Boston, 1949). Thomas C. De Leon's two reminiscences, *Four Years in Rebel Capitals* (Mobile, 1890) and *Belles, Beaux, and Brains of the Sixties* (New York, 1909) were eagerly read in the preparation of this study because the clerk of the Office of Provisions and Clothing was named T. C. De Leon. The author is commonly said to have been a clerk in the War Department, but his name appears on none of the available lists of that agency's employees. De Leon may have worked for the navy, but he had little to say about the navy in his books and nothing that would connect him with it. He generally approved of Mallory, highly praised Surgeon Spotswood, and failed to mention Paymaster De Bree of the Office of Provisions and Clothing.

Other diaries or reminiscences read included John B. Jones, *A Rebel War Clerk's Diary* (2 vols.; Philadelphia, 1866); Frank E. Vandiver, ed., *The Civil War Diary of Josiah Gorgas* (University, Ala., 1947); and Edward Younger, ed., *Inside the Confederate Government, the Diary of Robert G. H. Kean* (New York, 1957).

Howard K. Beale, ed., *Diary of Gideon Welles* (3 vols.; New York, 1960) contains valuable information on Union naval organization and related problems. Dunbar Rowland, ed., *Jefferson Davis Constitutionalist: His Letters, Papers, and Speeches* (10 vols., Jackson, Miss., 1923) has a few references to naval matters. The correspondence of Henry Graves and his brother Dutton Graves, respectively a marine lieutenant and a master's mate, appears in Richard Harwell, ed., *A Confederate Marine* (Tuscaloosa, 1963). These are good letters, intelligently written and useful for Marine Corps affairs and shipboard routine.

Biographies

Three biographies which today would be published with title pages listing the subject as co-authors or at least giving them "as told to" status were Diana Fontaine Maury Corbin, *A Life of Matthew Fontaine Maury* (London, 1888); Charles C. Jones, Jr., *The Life and Service of Commodore Josiah Tattnall* (Savannah, 1878); and Emma Maffitt, *Life and Service of John N. Maffitt* (New York, 1906). These are all anti-Mallory.

Stephen R. Mallory had no biographer at all for many years and need of a first-rate treatment of this strange man still exists. The only full length biography is Joseph T. Durkin, *Stephen H. Mallory* (Chapel Hill, 1954). This book leaves much to be desired, particularly in the discussion of Navy Department administration and Durkin's handling of Mallory's personality.

Brief biographical sketches of Mallory are included in Burton J. Hendrick, *Statesmen of the Lost Cause: Jefferson Davis and his Cabinet* (Boston, 1939) and Rembert W. Patrick, *Jefferson Davis and his Cabinet* (Baton Rouge, 1944). Neither book gives much space to matters of organization and administration, although both contain thorough discussions of policy and strategic direction. Both of these authorities conclude that Mallory achieved as much success as Secretary of the Confederate Navy as was possible under existing circumstances.

In Charles L. Lewis, *Admiral Franklin Buchanan* (Baltimore, 1939) are to be found a few wartime letters of Buchanan not printed elsewhere but the book contains disappointingly little material on naval organization.

Other Printed Works

John T. Scharf, *History of the Confederate States Navy* (New York, 1887), written by a former officer in the Confederate Navy, is rambling and sometimes inaccurate but is the only full-length treatment of the subject. Scharf accepted uncritically the statements of participants and is sometimes inconsistent. Much of the material Scharf used is not now available. His treatment of organizational matters is brief and generally unsatisfactory.

Robert U. Johnson and Clarence C. Buel, eds., *Battles and Leaders of the Civil War* (4 vols.; New York, 1882) has little material on the Confederate Navy. Volume twelve of Clement A. Evans, ed., *Confederate Military History* (12 vols.; Atlanta, 1899) contains an excellent piece on the Confederate Navy written by William H. Parker.

The best work on strategic and policy questions is Bern Anderson, *By Sea and by River* (New York, 1962). Admiral Anderson contributed much clear analytical thinking to his subject but his research was limited to *O.R.N.*

The finest work of scholarship used in the preparation of this study was James P. Baxter, *The Introduction of the Ironclad Warship* (Cambridge, 1933). From records in Europe as well as in this country, Baxter demonstrates that the *Merrimack-Monitor* duel was not nearly so revolutionary as is commonly believed; more than a hundred ironclads were under construction in 1861, and the naval arms race had its beginnings several years earlier.

Frank L. Owsley, *King Cotton Diplomacy* (Chicago, 1931) was especially useful in writing Chapter 20.

Periodicals

A number of articles on the Confederate Navy were found in Southern Historical Society *Papers*. The best of these were: Violet G. Alexander, "The Confederate States Navy Yard at Charlotte, N.C., 1862–65," XL (1915), 183–194; John M. Brooke, "The *Virginia* or *Merrimac*, Her Real Projector," XIX (1891),

3–34 [gives major credit to Mallory]; David B. Conrad, "The Capture of the C. S. Ram *Tennessee* in Mobile Bay, August 1864," XIX (1891), 72–82 [excellent on medical service aboard ship]; Hunter Davidson, "Electrical Torpedoes as a System of Defense," II (1876), 2; Gabriel J. Rains, "Torpedoes," III (1877), 256 [opposing views]; W. J. Glassell "Reminiscences of Torpedo Service in Charleston Harbor," IV (1878), 225–235; and George W. Gift, "The Story of the *Arkansas*," XII (1884), 48–54, 115–119, 163–170, 205–212 [an excellent article including much on construction, command relationship, and ship operations].

Walter W. Stephen, "The Brooke guns from Selma," *Alabama Historical Quarterly* XX (Fall, 1958), 462–475, has some interesting figures on ordnance production extracted from records of the Naval Ordnance Works.

Harrison A. Trexler, "The Confederate Navy Department and the Fall of New Orleans," *Southwestern Review* XIX (October, 1933), 88–102, is a well-written article based on the report of the investigation, *O.R.N.*, series 2, I.

Charles O. Paullin, "Naval Administration, 1842–1861," *Proceedings Of the United States Naval Institute* XXXIII (1907), 1435, 1448–77, provides excellent background for United States naval administration during the Civil War.

Index